Mark *my* Words

by Mark Schwarzer
with Mark Hooper

Photographic acknowledgements:
Blades Sports Photography, Highland Studios, Paul Thompson, Evening Gazette.

Published by:
Middlesbrough Football and Athletic Club (1986) Ltd, 1998.

Designed and printed by:
JW Northend Ltd, Sheffield.

Introduction

Looking back at the 1997-98 season, it was an amazing campaign. So much happened on and off the field. From the opening of pre-season training in July through to the final match in May, life was rarely dull.

It was an incredible season for me and the club. After relegation and two cup final defeats, as well as plenty of stories off the field in the 1996-97 season, another cup final was reached and promotion was secured on the last day of the season. There was plenty going on behind the scenes as well. With players like Fabrizio Ravanelli, Emerson, Paul Merson and Paul Gascoigne around, there's plenty of stories to tell.

Despite what some people might think though, a footballer's life isn't always glamorous and exciting. There are boring days which just involve training or getting treatment. So rather than make a diary entry every day, this book records my thoughts as the weeks, months and matches went by over the season.

Hopefully by reading this book you'll see a bit of what life is like as a professional footballer. Everyone is different and this is my personal story.

chapter one

Pre-Season

Don't get me wrong, I hate pre-season training. But I would much rather be out putting myself through agony than doing what I am doing now. Instead, I'm holed up at home with my leg in plaster and facing a lengthy rehabilitation before I can get back to playing football.

It's July 3rd, 1997 and my Middlesbrough team-mates are reporting back at the club for pre-season training, preparing for the new season. It's less than two months since the double disappointment of relegation from the Premier League and defeat in two cup finals but we have to raise ourselves for another vital season.

We've all had time to go away and mull things over and try and work out where it all went wrong last season. At least now we have the chance to make amends by bouncing back at the first attempt. It's a big challenge and will by no means be easy but I think, with a bit of strengthening here and there, we can do it.

But I'm not with the lads as they get down to the hard work of making up for two months sitting on a beach. I've been out for a few months with a leg injury that has turned into a personal nightmare.

The injury actually happened in a game against West Ham towards the end of last season, just after the Coca-Cola Cup Final against Leicester. It was a frustrating game, 0-0, and late on I was caught as I was taking a cross. One of their players, Marc Rieper, caught me with his knee or his foot and spun me round.

I realised straight away that it was something more serious than just a knock. I've seen it on TV since and I think it was mostly frustration on his part. It was a game they needed to win. We had games in hand and they were still in danger of going down. All game I was coming out and collecting crosses. They were getting frustrated and I think because of that he just went right through me. He had absolutely no chance of getting the ball. I stayed on for another 10 minutes and even kicked a few more balls. My leg nearly fell off! I could tell something was wrong but no-one was sure how bad the damage was.

After the game I was struggling, I couldn't walk. At that particular time I had to pick a new car up. I'd organised to stay down in London, collect the car and drive it back up north. I stayed the night at my agent, Barry Silkman's, house in London and then drove the car right the way up to Middlesbrough. It was my right leg that was injured and, as you can imagine, it was a nightmare trying to drive. I shouldn't have done it. With hindsight, it was a stupid thing to do. The club's physio Bob Ward and everybody else at the club knew I was driving back up north but nobody thought it was serious and I just did it. Bob thought the injury was just a knock. He didn't think it was broken and nor did the doctor. But the way it felt, when I moved my leg it was as if I could feel the bone moving the other way. It was a funny feeling.

I went for an X-ray at the Friarage hospital in Northallerton the next day. I was a passenger in Bob's car and, as we turned round a corner, I held my leg down and could feel the bottom part of my leg moving out a bit. I could feel there was something wrong but nothing really showed on the X-rays. It was only a few days later when a specialist looked at the X-rays and noticed a crack.

2

With an X-ray it obviously depends on the angle of the picture and if it's cracked on the other side you don't really see it.

The worst thing was that, before they found the crack, the club had been trying to get me fit. The incident happened on the Wednesday night and at the weekend we were playing against Chesterfield in the FA Cup semi-final. I knew I couldn't play in that game but they tried to get me fit for the following week when we had a replay of the Coca-Cola Cup Final against Leicester.

For the first three or four days I could hardly walk on my leg. I was in the hotel with the team at Mottram Hall before the Chesterfield game and Bob got me into an ice bath. The movement was coming back in my leg and things felt OK but it still wasn't quite right. It was Monday or Tuesday when I found out there was a fracture. The doctor had left a message on Bob's answering machine to say he'd found it.

But even after that, nobody thought it was really serious. I had a couple of days not doing much and then tried to get fit again. I tried training as we built up to the Tottenham game a couple of days later. I travelled down to London and trained with the team. Looking back I think that's when I really aggravated the injury. It was just a crack but then I think there was a clean break right through. It felt OK during the training session but I couldn't take any crosses so I had to stop.

That night they put me on the bench as a precautionary measure. Ben Roberts was playing but Gary Walsh was also out with a broken finger and I was there as cover. It's a good job I didn't have to go on. I don't think playing with a broken leg is the best idea! It would have been hopeless, I couldn't even run, let alone kick the ball.

After that, they told me to leave it and rest. I couldn't walk for three or four days again. It was horrendous. Everyone felt that we didn't need to put the leg in plaster. With the benefit of hindsight everyone looks back and says "We should have plastered it, shouldn't we" but they decided it wasn't necessary.

There were only about five or six weeks of the season to go at that stage so, because it was broken right the way through, they said that was it for the rest of the season. As we were coming towards the end of the campaign I had another X-ray to make sure everything was lined up properly. No problems showed up so they said: "Go away on holiday and forget about it all".

Originally I'd planned to go back to Australia and I'd also been called up to play for the Australian national team but I decided not to go home and pulled out of the internationals. Instead, I went to Spain with my girlfriend Paloma for four weeks. I lay on the beach, sat in the apartment, swam, walked down to the beach - did the usual lazy, holiday stuff. But it wasn't getting better, I could walk without a considerable limp but I couldn't run. I could swim but I could still feel it a little bit. It was hurting.

Then, about three weeks into the holiday, I received a phone call on my mobile from the club's goalkeeping coach Mike Kelly asking me how I was. I told him it didn't look good at all, I couldn't even run yet. He said that we were starting pre-season training in about three weeks' time so I'd better speak to Bob Ward. I rang Bob straight away and he told me to come back over. I organised another flight and headed back.

As soon as I arrived I had another X-ray. It was then that I was told the bone had shifted out of place. The specialist couldn't believe it, he said he'd never seen anything like it before. He actually uses my X-rays now for some of his lectures, because it's so unusual for a fibula to react as mine had. It had moved out of place. It was hanging on each side, trying to grow back, but had stopped at one point as there was no joining of the bones. Because it had stopped healing, they ended up operating and putting in a plate of about 10 cm long and 2 mm thick with eight screws. They tell me it will be in until next summer so now it depends on whether Australia qualify for the World Cup. If we do and I'm selected then it will be taken out afterwards so I would miss the start of next season or pre-season at least.

The operation was on June 24th. I was in hospital for four days and then I was told to go home and rest for two weeks. That's what I'm doing now. Then I will start on the slow road to recovery. It looks like it will be a couple of months before I can get back to playing and it will a be a difficult and frustrating time.

I have to say I'm very disappointed with the way things have turned out and it is difficult to handle. I don't blame anyone personally but it's annoying that the injury has dragged on so long and been so difficult to diagnose.

The one good thing is that I'm glad it didn't happen when I was at my former club Bradford City. Back then, I didn't have the status I have now. I'd just come over from playing in Germany and nobody knew who I was.

There were things said at Bradford, like that I was bought for £350,000 when it was really only £150,000. They were trying to bump the price up to say the club had invested a lot of money in me. After five or six games there was already talk in the paper about other clubs being interested in me. It was one of those things you hear all the time as a player but it came very soon.

No disrespect to Bradford, because I had a great time there, but I was pleased in many ways because my main goal was to come over here, play as few games as possible in the First Division to prove myself and then get into a Premier League team.

I felt that in the first 16 games at Bradford and the 11 games last season at Middlesbrough that I'd proven myself enough. I felt the security there with the gaffer and the team. I felt that the team were confident in me and the fans as well.

Another thing that makes this lay-off harder to take is just being relegated. You could say I'm accustomed to it because, before moving to England, the two clubs I played for in Germany were both relegated. But I never really played in those teams. I played two games for my first club, Dynamo Dresden, and then at Kaiserslautern I took part in only four games in the whole season so it wasn't as if I was really part of it. It was a big shock for Kaiserslautern though as, until then, they were one of only three clubs never to have been relegated from the Bundesliga.

It was much more difficult for me at Middlesbrough. Things had been going well up until the injury and the team went on a great run. It did coincide with my arrival but there was a marked improvement all round. We all believed that we would get out of relegation and, looking back, I think the real turning point was the Coca-Cola Cup Final. I think we would have stayed up had we won that.

We were on such a run, such a high before the game but it took a lot out of us. If you look at it, for the last 15 or 20 games Middlesbrough were in unbelievable form. We played five or six games at one stage around March and we won four, drew one and lost one. The one we lost was the second leg against Stockport in the Coca-Cola semi and that didn't matter because we were two up from the away leg.

The only other defeat I played in was against Sheffield Wednesday at the beginning of March. That was my first Premier League game and it was a nightmare. I honestly thought "What have I done here? Who have I transferred to now?" We were hopeless. It was a pretty tough initiation to Premier League football for me. Fortunately, that game seemed miles away from what followed.

My actual debut came a few days before that in the Coca-Cola semi-final first leg against Stockport. It never really hit me that it was a semi-final. It was only after the second leg a few weeks later, when the crowd called us back out at the Riverside and everyone was talking about the club getting to a major final for the first time.

But the cup wasn't the reason I signed. I signed to be in the Premier League. When I joined we only had 19 points. We were four points behind the team above and eight behind a safe spot. I don't know what I was thinking!

I looked at the team and thought there must be a reason for being in the position we were. As soon as I arrived I knew there was something wrong in the dressing room. I could sense the ill feeling about particular players. There were definitely factions within the dressing room and it was affecting the team spirit.

In the end, it all came down to the last game of the season at Leeds. Before the game, I really thought we'd win. Everyone was confident. Then in the match, we had so many chances and just didn't score. It was only after Brian Deane scored for them that Juninho got a goal. We really should have won the game.

In the dressing room after the game, you could hear a pin drop. It's not the nicest thing to happen and it didn't make it any easier for me having suffered it twice before, being relegated on the last day.

It was incredibly frustrating. I knew that just a few weeks before things had been going really well. Of course, I didn't want to be back playing in the First Division.

The worst thing was it should never have come that far. There was a lot of talk about the fact that we should have played the game against Blackburn before Christmas when the club called off the match because of an injury and illness crisis. We were deducted three points by the FA and in the end it turned out that with those three points we would have stayed up. We could have played Blackburn and lost 10-0 or 15-0 and still been in the Premier League. Some of the players were thinking that. But we should never have been in that position anyway. The team was good enough to stay up and didn't perform well enough over the whole season.

I'm not the only one not to make it back for pre-season training. But at least I've got a good excuse! Fabrizio Ravanelli has failed to report in and it's no big surprise to me. The general feeling is that we couldn't care less whether he comes back or not, just that it's all sorted out. I'm not sure it would be fair to blame him for all the club's problems last season but he certainly played a big part. I could tell there was ill feeling towards him when I first joined the club. There's always been togetherness between groups of the players but not as a whole team.

When you know everyone is giving 100 per cent, everyone fights for one another. Last season there were times when Rav was not happy about things and he showed it by putting his hands up in the air and abusing people, going towards the bench and shouting "take him off". People hear that and it sets off bad vibes. People wonder: "Why am I running my arse off for this idiot when he's slagging me off?"

My own personal relationship with Rav has never gone further than saying "hello" and "goodbye" and so on. Last season, he spoke to me very little, as he did with everyone else. The only one he really spoke to was Gianluca Festa because of the Italian connection.

The first big transfer news of the new season is the signing of Paul Merson from Arsenal. I don't know a tremendous amount about him but my biggest memory, probably like everyone else, is of the day he went on television and admitted he was a drug addict, gambler and alcoholic. Of course, I've seen him playing for Arsenal but, coming from Australia and over in Germany, he's known a lot more for that press conference than for his playing. I must admit that I hope he's over all these problems because we really need stability at the moment after what happened last season.

Merson's arrival has coincided with the departure of last season's player of the year Juninho. He's signed for Atletico Madrid for £12 million. It's a tremendous fee for the club and a frightening amount of money. The club would have been crazy to turn it down. Spanish clubs seem to be prepared to pay any amount of money for top players.

It was one of those things where the majority of the players were saying we've got to let him go. There was certainly no ill feeling towards him whatsoever. If anyone did feel ill feeling they would be incredibly selfish. He always gave 150 per cent. And I don't think he would have been right for the First Division. You look at Manchester City last season with Georgi Kinkladze and, though he is a world class player, I think they would have been better off without him.

Last year, if anyone was under pressure with the ball, we'd just think give it to Juninho, let him do the work. We can't make the same mistake this season with Merson. Everybody has to take their own share of the responsibility.

It's sad that Juninho's going but he's been as good as threatened by the Brazilian coach that he has to leave if he wants to play for his country. I think he's done the right thing. Spain is the ideal league for him as a player and even with the language and the climate, it will be better for him.

Juninho came back to complete the deal and a lot of the boys were disappointed that he didn't say goodbye. Everyone had a bit of a laugh though about the street fight he got into while he was over. He wasn't hurt but it was all over the papers that he'd been hit by some guy because he'd been seeing his girlfriend. I can't imagine Juninho fighting back. Being a single lad and so popular, Juninho did have girls throwing themselves at him and he's not to know whether they had a boyfriend or not. Sometimes things like that happen when you're not careful enough!

Another big change over the summer, especially for me, is the departure of the goalkeeping coach Mike Kelly to Nottingham Forest. It happened when I was in hospital having my operation. When I saw it on Teletext, I couldn't believe it. I was really shocked and disappointed. I had no idea he was going to leave.

Mike had a lot to do with me coming to Middlesbrough in the first place. The club often asked him to check out different 'keepers and apparently there's a few times when they've gone to Mike and asked: "Is this 'keeper good?" and he's said no. But with me, he went to the gaffer and said: "I want him". Here I am.

He came down and watched me play once at Crystal Palace. As it happens, we lost the game 3-1 and the manager Chris Kamara tried to blame me for two of the goals. I couldn't believe it and neither could anyone else. Mike must have liked what he saw.

I didn't know anything about Mike before I came to Middlesbrough but Martin Hunter, the assistant trainer at Bradford, used to work at the Football Association. He knew Mike through Mike's time with England when Terry Venables was in charge. Martin said Mike was one of the best in the country.

I really enjoyed working with him. There were a few people who didn't like him too much, but you don't have to like someone to work with them. I didn't have that problem because I liked him and we got on well. He wasn't an easy person for some to get along with but I had no problems whatsoever.

After missing the first couple of weeks of pre-season recuperating at home, I'm back at the club starting treatment. It's nice to get back to it after having the plaster on my leg. I've played lots of computer games and watched a lot of TV. I don't play the sort of games on the Nintendo that David James used to, the ones he blamed for losing a game at Middlesbrough last season. But I'm really hooked on the PC football management games. I'm managing Bradford City now and it's 2008, I'm in the Premier League and I've got £18 million in the bank!

I'm not really seeing the other players because the club's new training ground hasn't been finished. I have to come to the stadium for treatment. The machines I need are still at the stadium so I'm coming in seven days a week to work with one of the physios, Gary Henderson.

The team has just come back from 10 days in Italy and they're going to be spending seven days playing some games in Northern Ireland so I'm hardly seeing any of them. It's a funny build-up because I don't feel part of it. I don't know how training is going except from what I've heard from Mikkel Beck. I keep in contact with him quite a bit.

I'm not disappointed to have missed the Italy trip. I hate going away to train and hopefully when our training ground is completed we won't need to do it. I'd much rather train twice a day here and go back to my own home.

The theory behind trips like these is building team spirit. I don't think that's right when it's a pre-season trip because everyone gets so tired that there isn't much time for socialising. A lot of players are sour-faced because it's a hard time of the season so everyone just wants to get it over with. I don't find it a real morale booster.

Apparently it was a nice place in Italy and the restaurant there was good but apart from that it wasn't the best. The boys tell me the training pitches were appalling. It was supposed to be Juventus' training ground and there was one bit that Juve use but we weren't allowed on it!

On the way back, the lads caught up with our old friend, Fabrizio Ravanelli. It was an amazing coincidence that he was on the same flight from Milan to Manchester. He was flying over to England to have transfer talks with Everton. Apparently, he walked past all the players and got on the plane. He completely blanked everyone apart from the gaffer, Bryan Robson, and Viv Anderson. Everyone is incredibly annoyed by it and hopes it's the last we will see of him.

It's been announced that the club has a season ticket sell-out for the coming season. It makes me feel fantastic to know that every game at the Riverside will be a 30,000 full house. When I heard, my first reaction was to shake my head and think that the supporters must be crazy! There can't be many clubs that can count on that kind of support having just been relegated. They are incredible and it's a massive boost to everyone at the club to know they are behind us.

The support last season was brilliant. It really makes a difference and the Riverside should be an imposing place for visiting teams this season. I don't think we'll lose too many games with that kind of atmosphere. It just goes to show that it's right that football supporters in the North-East are fanatical.

The only explanation is that the club is so ambitious and people have responded to that. The chairman Steve Gibson has put his money where his mouth is. Not that you hear from him too often. I never even met him until two months after I signed. I've always been used to presidents in Germany, who don't own the club but are the figureheads, and they are all show-ponies, desperate for attention. The chairmen over here are much more the bosses because they own the clubs but you don't see them as much. There are exceptions but Steve Gibson stays out of the limelight. If someone has a lot of money and wants to invest it in football that's great for the sport and he has turned Middlesbrough round. The fans have responded to what he has done behind the scenes and he is a big hero with them.

Ravanelli has finally reported back at the club after his move to Everton fell through. The papers are saying that he asked for ridiculous amounts of money and 28 free flights back to Italy among other things. I certainly wouldn't put it past him. Everton are desperate and he thought he could demand what he liked but I'm not surprised they turned him down.

Throughout last season it was said in the papers that Rav was on £42,000 a week. You can't believe everything you read in the papers but people have asked whether that causes friction among the players and it does with me - I wonder why my agent hasn't got that much for me! But, to be fair, there's no point worrying about what other players are on. If you do that you will just drive yourself crazy, you've just got to be satisfied with what you're on. There's always someone on more money than you. It's a little bit different when you play in the same position as someone who has similar ability and experience to you but they're on much more money. But there's no comparison between a central defender and a striker who scores 31 goals a season.

People also ask whether it causes friction to have foreign players earning much more than the English ones. But that's always the case wherever you go in the world. I suppose it's because foreigners that come in are, generally, internationals and playing for top international teams like Brazil, Italy or

Germany. If you want world class players, you have to pay world class wages. In any case, I would never discuss my wages with another player and no-one's ever asked me. If people did start discussing it - and people do exaggerate - that would cause friction.

There's certainly a lot of resentment among the team now about Rav coming back. How can someone treat the club the way he has, state publicly that he doesn't want to play for Middlesbrough anymore and then come back? It also comes on the back of the FA Cup Final when there was a confrontation between Rav and Neil Cox before the game, which all the players and the supporters knew about.

Some of the boys have made a few comments to him but he either didn't understand them or chose to ignore them. The reaction was actually quite tame compared to some places I've been to, considering what's happened. I played in Germany for two and a half years and the discipline is much more severe over there. If anyone ever did what Rav has done to a club in Germany, no matter who they were, he would never ever come back again. The club would make him sit it out until they got the money they wanted for him. We feel a bit let down by the club, letting him come back.

With only a week to go before the start of the season, I've finally moved up to the club's new training ground, Rockliffe Park, in the village of Hurworth. It's early days at the moment but I'm impressed with the plans I've seen for it when they construct all the buildings. It's hard to visualise but it has amazing potential. At the moment, we're using temporary buildings but there's a tremendous old hall as you go in and then there's plenty of room for pitches and all the other facilities.

I only experienced the previous training facilities, at Tollesby Road in Middlesbrough, for a couple of months. They certainly weren't Premier League standard, or even First Division, but the club has obviously had it in mind to move to better facilities.

Bradford had a similar set-up to what we had at Middlesbrough last season. It was poor and you had to travel from the stadium to the pitches. Both clubs I was at in Germany had good facilities right next to their stadiums. It was a big shock going to Bradford but I always saw that as a stepping stone and was happy to put up with it. I was a bit surprised that Middlesbrough didn't have better facilities but the gaffer told me about the plans.

The only problem is that the pitches at the moment at Rockliffe are a nightmare. It's quite dangerous in places, with rocks and uneven sections, but hopefully it will settle down. I'm not actually training on the pitches yet, that's a few weeks away, but I'm doing some running.

Peter Shilton has been appointed as the new goalkeeping coach and, having met him, he seems a nice guy. When I first heard that he was replacing Mike Kelly, I was a bit apprehensive because I'd heard some things about Peter as a trainer before that weren't so good. It's a couple of weeks until I can start training with him so I'll have to wait and see.

Funnily enough, though he's a legend in this country, I was never a great fan of him as a player. His record speaks for itself but he never really stood out for me. The only 'keeper I remember liking as a kid was Jean Marie Pfaff from Belgium.

Rav has been the centre of attention again after getting involved in a scuffle on the training ground with Curtis Fleming. It was all a bit familiar after what happened with Neil Cox last season.

It all goes back to an interview Curtis gave after we played Blackburn near the end of last season. We drew 0-0 in a game we really needed to win and some of the local media asked about Rav, who had gone back to Italy for treatment on an injury. Curtis said he should have been there with the team, not back in

Italy. Unfortunately, the quotes were taken and put out nationally. Curtis probably regretted saying anything and not keeping it within the club, but I could understand his frustration because Rav had regularly said things about the other players and had got away with it by saying that he'd been misquoted.

Most of this happened before I joined the club. He would make comments in the Italian media and then when he came back he'd say he'd been misquoted. But I can't believe you can be misquoted 20 or 30 times. Papers would be out of business - they'd be sued like you wouldn't believe.

Rav and Curtis were never friends but Rav remembered what Curtis had said and had a go at him. I wasn't there but obviously you hear about it from the other players. It wasn't a major incident but no doubt it will get into the papers somehow.

I've only seen it twice before at both the clubs in Germany where players have had a coming together. It doesn't happen too often but it's only natural, things like that are going to happen when you've got a big group of young lads almost living together. It's like in a school classroom. You're always going to have people who don't get on and you get little cliques.

Some people were surprised about the amount of media coverage the club received last season but, with players of the calibre of Ravanelli, Emerson and Juninho, you've got to expect it really. Even Manchester United, Arsenal and so on weren't getting the coverage we were but when you've got Rav complaining all the time, Emmo going AWOL, Juninho playing brilliantly as well as things like the Premier League and the three points issue, then you have to expect it.

For me, the way to avoid it is not to read the papers. If you just ignore it, it can't get to you. People are just writing what they think. If you read the papers, in each there's guaranteed to be six or seven different stories. You can't believe all the speculation.

But I think a lot of players do read papers. Some people don't need to read about themselves in the paper, some do. It's a showbiz world now and some people thrive on media attention. I generally only read the papers if they are in the dressing room or lying around at the training ground. I don't run down to the paper shop after a game to see how many marks out of 10 I got!

As we get ready to start the season, Merson is the only new face at the club. We've been linked with loads of other players like Ian Wright, David Platt, Dean Sturridge and a fair few others but nothing has come of it.

With my injury, the club brought the Welsh international Andy Dibble in on trial for pre-season. He played in a few games but with two other 'keepers in Ben Roberts and Gary Walsh, and me, hopefully, not being too far away from fitness, the gaffer has let him go.

The former Spanish international Jose Maria Bakero has also been on trial. Mikkel roomed with him and said he was a nice guy with tremendous skills but I think the club thought he wasn't right for the English league and especially the first division so we didn't take him on.

I'm not surprised there's no-one else come in. It was bound to be difficult to get players to come here. No-one knows how much players have been put off by the reputation the club had last season for off-the-field problems and it can't help with someone like Ravanelli still being at the club. It was nowhere near as bad as people made out last year but it's understandable that people are put off by what was written in the papers.

Another thing is that everyone knows it is very hard, when you've just got relegated, to pick yourself up and get promoted straight away. The good thing is that we haven't lost too many players and we definitely have enough quality to go back up.

I think Nottingham Forest and Sunderland are going to be our main rivals. They'll have the same problem as us having just come down but I think they're both strong sides and look to have made some decent signings. Otherwise, Wolves and Sheffield United would be my other bets. United had a good season last year and have some useful players, as do Wolves.

chapter two

Early Season

Charlton were the first opponents of the new season and we were very lucky to beat them. We went behind but Luca Festa pulled one back and we got a fortunate winner late on from Ravanelli. It wasn't the most confident and impressive of openings but at least we got off to a winning start.

After last season, losing two cup finals and going down on the last day, it's easy to see why it's going to be hard for us to go straight back up. It was so close to being an unbelievable season but ended up being a complete disaster. I think a lot of players haven't got a grip of reality in this division yet and there's still a hangover from last season.

Having missed most of pre-season and then going back to Italy again for a few days just before the start, apparently to sort out a driving licence, it has naturally caused a bit of tension among the boys to see Ravanelli starting the first game of the season. But you couldn't argue with the fact that he scored the goal that won us the game. A few people said that he had been booed by the crowd but I thought they were actually very good to him. Most of them were still behind him.

I hate watching our games from the stands. It's really frustrating and when we play like we did against Charlton I'm tearing my hair out. I feel like yelling out and abusing people but you get some funny looks. In a game you can stand in the goal and scream out but you can't in the grandstand.

I'm not a full-on shouter on the pitch like some 'keepers, I do try to be constructive. I don't like putting people down because I had it happen to me in Germany. I didn't like it and I'm sure other people don't. Sometimes you need to tell people something but there's a right way to do it. You need to let people know players are behind them and so on.

I'm finally back in training and it's hard to know if you're doing enough. I'm hardly doing anything with my legs at all. I'm doing most of it on my own and I don't know how far to push myself. I don't think there's a danger of doing myself any damage because I want to be sure. A few more weeks is better than putting myself out for another six months.

It has been scary because I wondered if I was ever going to be fit. It was hard to see a light at the end of the tunnel. I honestly wondered if I was ever going to walk without limping. I'm not the sort of person who lets life get me down though. I had some tough times out in Germany and coming through those has helped me.

The papers are all full of stories about Rio Ferdinand, the young West Ham defender. He's been dropped from the England squad for their game against Moldova by Glenn Hoddle because he got caught drink-driving.

It all brings back memories of a similar experience for me in October 1994. It was during my first six months in Germany with Dynamo Dresden. I was 22 at the time, out of my country for the first time by myself and it wasn't the easiest circumstances at the club. I wasn't looked after as well as I would have hoped. Dresden is a beautiful place but it's not that modern. Being in the old East Germany, there aren't the shops or anything else like the old West. But I do like the place and I still have property and a lot of friends there.

One night, I went out, had a few drinks and then drove home. I don't know why I did it but it's something I regret. I fell asleep at the wheel and smashed up my car. I wrote it off. Thank God, nobody was injured but I ended up in court. I was fined 30,000 Deutsch Marks and suspended from driving for a year.

Dynamo Dresden weren't impressed and kicked me out straight away. We had just got a new trainer, Horst Hrubsch, a few days before. I had done really well in training and he seemed to like me. Things were starting to look up after what had been a difficult start and then I went and did something really stupid like that.

It made me realise how dangerous drink-driving is. There's people that do it all the time and I must admit I used to do it a bit in Australia. You always think you can get away with it. But you learn from it and I'm sure Ferdinand will. It's a hard lesson but I learnt from it.

The coach eventually got me back into the club. The president, Rolf Jurgen Otto, didn't speak to me for a few months until I played some good games and he knew he could sell me for some money. Then he was my best friend again. He was a bit of a loony anyway. In the end, he got put in jail for three years for financial irregularities. It was a very strange club.

Dresden signed me for 300,000 Australian dollars (about £150,000) from Marconi. I played two games in the one season when I was there. I was number two to the Russian national 'keeper Stanislav Cherchesov. He went away for national games and I came in for those. I played really well but as soon as Cherchesov came back I lost my place.

The club was relegated that season and then lost its licence to play in the Second Division, which is a professional league, and went down to the Third. The president was charged with fraud and he basically ran the club millions of Deutsch Marks into the red. They had to sell most of their players to raise money. The president offered me a lot of money to stay on but, within a couple of weeks, he was in jail and I turned his offer down. Then they sold me to Kaiserslautern for 550,000 Deutsch Marks (about £170,000).

I chose to leave Australia and move to Germany in the first place because I have dual German and Australian nationality. At the time, there was the three foreigner rule in operation so it would have been very difficult to join any other European club but, with my German passport, that was the place to go.

Both my parents were born in Germany. Dad was born in the East, in Zwickau, but was brought up in the West, near Stuttgart. My mother's from Baaden Baaden. They got married in 1966 and, at the time, three different countries - South Africa, Argentina and Australia - were asking people to move out. The governments paid for boat trips on the condition that you stayed for two years.

Before they got married, my father told my mother they were going away. He said if you're staying then we're not getting married. Obviously she said OK, but that she wanted to come back after the two years. My father said "we'll see what happens". He applied for the three countries and said "which ever one comes back first, we'll go." Luckily it was Australia. Otherwise, I could be trying to get into the South African or Argentinean sides now - or walking down the streets with a gun in my pocket! They had to live in certain areas and it was difficult, but my father loved it and they settled in Sydney.

My father was actually coach of the junior team I played for in Australia as a kid. It was him that turned me into a 'keeper because I really wanted to play on pitch. Nobody would go in goal and he threw me in. He says now that it was because I kept falling over my feet but I can't believe that!

Our second game of the season ended in disaster with a 1-0 defeat against Stoke. They aren't anything special but we were awful and deserved to lose. Anyone who thinks we're going to walk the First Division and get back in the Premier League must realise now that it is going to be really hard.

We are going to have to adjust to the First Division and sometimes grind out results. The First Division and Premier League are miles apart. It's a totally different way of playing football. There's so much more skill involved in the Premier League. The crosses are harder and more precise and the finishing is more accurate. The First Division is a hell of a lot more physical, a lot more kick and rush.

I don't think 'keepers suffer any more because of that physical side. You get challenges going in but I got that in the Premier League. I remember against Nottingham Forest when I was clattered by Pierre Van Hooijdonk. He came through and elbowed me in the back of the head - it was the first time I ever saw stars! The ref and linesman never even saw it. Then in the same game, I was lying on the floor with the ball and Stuart Pearce studded me between the legs! There are times when you can't look after yourself because you're watching the ball and players hit you from behind, as Van Hooijdonk did, and you've got no chance. For a goalkeeper it's probably easier in the First Division because there's a lot less power and accuracy on the crosses.

I've always said, even when I was back in Australia, that England is the best league in the world for goalkeepers and strikers. It's one of the only leagues in the world where they really emphasise having good goalkeepers. What really surprises me about England is that there aren't many goalkeepers that come off their line and take crosses. People are surprised when I come out and take crosses all the time. I think it's just part of the game. It's not just my height, though it helps being 6'4", it's all about footwork and timing. You look at Dave Beasant, he's taller than me, but he never looks comfortable with crosses.

You also look at the top English 'keepers like Kevin Pressman and Nigel Martyn, even David Seaman, they aren't the best with crosses. Paul Merson was telling me that they call David Seaman "Dracula" at Arsenal! I think that's why Bruce

Grobbelaar was so well liked in this country. He always came out - he missed a lot but he stood out because he would go for them.

There are a lot of foreign goalkeepers now in this country and there are plenty of my fellow Aussies. There's Mark Bosnich at Aston Villa, John Filan at Blackburn, Jason Kearton, who was at Everton and now plays for Crewe, and also Zeljko Kalac, who was at Leicester. Terry Venables is looking at taking him to Portsmouth.

Kalac is seen as one of my main rivals for the national team. Bosnich is considered the number one but I'm hoping to try and challenge him once I'm fit. It's going to be difficult being in the First Division for me to contest the number one jersey but I think I've got a good chance of being number two with the World Cup coming next summer. It's definitely a goal to play in the World Cup but my main aim is to play well for my club and hopefully that will follow.

I spoke to the coach, Terry Venables, quite a bit before the qualifiers in Australia in the summer. We spoke several times about my injury but I haven't heard from him since. The gaffer here, Bryan Robson, knows him from their time together coaching the England squad.

My only worry is that Venables might bare a grudge over something that happened last season. Just after I signed for Middlesbrough, I was down to make my debut in the second leg of the Coca-Cola Cup semi-final last season against Stockport. I had been called up for the national squad for a friendly but, as I wouldn't have played anyway, I asked if I could pull out.

At first, everything seemed fine. But a couple of days before the game, Venables rang me and said he wasn't happy with it. I told him that, as I'd just moved to Middlesbrough and it was a huge game for the club, I wanted to play for them. It was only a friendly. He said I had to make a decision, so I told him I was playing for Middlesbrough. When the next squad was announced I had been dropped. The issue hasn't arisen since and Venables was fine when I spoke with him but it will be interesting to see what happens when I'm fit.

I'm waiting to see what Venables does when the next friendly against Tunisia is played. I won't be fit but it clashes with Aston Villa's game against Bordeaux in the UEFA Cup. It will be interesting to see if Bosnich gets away with pulling out. I'll be amazed if he doesn't.

I've only trained with Venables for two days. The biggest difference he has made is to our profile. He's come in at a very fortunate time because we have so many good players playing in different countries. Australian players are getting better all the time and I would fancy our chances of getting to the World Cup whoever the manager was.

Over in Australia, people still rave about the 1974 team that reached the World Cup Finals in Germany. But that team doesn't compare to now. We have so many players that are playing at the top level around the world. We are definitely good enough to get to the World Cup Finals.

A lot of the players have come over to England and the fact that Venables is English and still involved in football here, as chairman of Portsmouth, has brought a lot of players over here. Quite a few seem to have joined Portsmouth, funnily enough. It all seems a bit strange after what happened to the former national coach, Eddie Thomson. He was the subject of a big two year inquiry in Australia about his involvement in player transfers. He was hounded about it. But when they held an inquiry into Terry Venables about all these players he has brought over to Portsmouth, it only took two days and he was cleared. It seems a bit of a conflict of interests to me.

I'm really disappointed to have missed the game against my old club Bradford. I missed playing in a pre-season friendly there and I've now had to miss the league game at the Pulse Stadium as well. Fortunately, we came away with a point after a 2-2 draw. Young Anthony Ormerod capped a great debut by scoring an excellent goal to equalise.

Bradford have had a good start to the season and their manager Chris Kamara has done very well there. I always got on well with him and he did a lot for me. I'm not sure whether he had the trust or belief in me or whether he was just desperate for a goalkeeper but he only saw me playing once in a reserve game against Bradford while I was on trial at Manchester City, and he bought me. He's not the sort of guy who you would want to get on the wrong side of - he does jump the gun a little bit sometimes - but he's only young as a manager.

Bryan Robson is a lot quieter than Chris and can keep his cool a bit easier. Bryan's a lot more relaxed. But in the dressing room behind closed doors, he can sometimes let loose. Even last year, he never seemed to be under that much pressure even though he was bitterly disappointed with the relegation.

When Middlesbrough and Everton came in with their offers, Chris was very good with me. He's from Middlesbrough himself and he said, if I was asking for his advice, he would recommend me to go to Middlesbrough.

There were other players there who had played for Middlesbrough themselves - Nicky Mohan, Richard Liburd and Tommy Wright - and I spoke to all of them. Chris Waddle was also there then and he said he would go to Middlesbrough.

I remember going to meet Bryan and Viv Anderson at the Four Seasons Hotel in Manchester. I was in awe of seeing Bryan Robson. I went with my girlfriend Paloma and asked her: "Do you know who this guy is?" She thought it was Bobby Robson but I said: "No, Bryan Robson, Manchester United, England." I couldn't believe I was meeting him.

He's still a great player in training now. He looks as good as a lot of players and very strong. I don't think he'll play unless there's a real emergency but he could still definitely do a job.

Andy Townsend has joined the club from Aston Villa. He's a really experienced player and has played at the top level for a long time. He should strengthen up our midfield. He's been captain at Villa and also of Republic of Ireland so he should be a good leader as well on the pitch.

Unfortunately, his debut at Tranmere has been overshadowed, yet again, by Ravanelli. He's gone back to Italy and didn't play. The gaffer has said that he's let him go back early because he's playing for Italy next week but I also think he'd just had enough of him. All the boys are glad that the gaffer has finally lost patience with him. Bryan has been more than fair with him.

Since he came back, Rav has been terrible around the club. He would come in to train, not speak to anyone and, within two minutes of the end, he was gone. One night, a couple of the boys were in a pub when Rav walked in. He looked up, saw them and put his head down and walked past them. He didn't seem interested in playing at all and we all knew that the only way it would get settled was if he left. He's clearly unhappy but there's right and wrong ways to go about things.

For the first game of the season, against Charlton, everybody bit the bullet and got on with the game with him but now he's ended up going again. This time, there's no way he can come back. Before he went, he was saying to one or two players that he was going and he wouldn't be playing in the Tranmere game. Then he just went. He's been taking the Mickey out of the club and it just shows a total lack of respect for his team-mates.

We're a few weeks into the season but it's all a bit flat around the club. There's no buzz at the moment, even with packed houses at the stadium. We haven't set the world alight with our form but we're not losing too many. You don't want to lose touch with the teams at the top but with games in hand, we're in a decent position. I'm just looking forward to getting back to playing football again.

chapter three

The Comeback

Since the game at Bradford, the lads have narrowly beaten Barnet in the second round of the Coca-Cola Cup and won 3-1 at home against Birmingham. We're still only mid-table in the league but things seem to be slowly falling into place. I nearly fell over in shock when I walked out at the Riverside for the Barnet game. There was less than 10,000 people there. I've never seen the stadium without it being completely sold out and I'm so used to it that I was really taken aback.

I'm now ready to the extent that I can train to full capacity and play, probably 98 per cent fit. I'm really close. There's a few aches and pains but I'm down to play in the second leg of the Barnet cup tie and I can't wait to get back out there.

I've worked hard in the last two months, going to the club and then to the Springs health club five or six times a week, on my own. It's hard to motivate yourself but it will be worth it when I get back on the pitch.

I've been training with Peter Shilton and he's working me pretty hard. Now I'm working with him, I'm impressed. He's still amazingly sharp for his age and got great handling. Peter was always known as a hard worker and that shows. He's only with us two days a week but we carry on for about an hour after all the other players have finished and it's hard work.

There's different exercises we do but in general there's only a few things you can do with goalkeepers. The principles are the same, there's just different ways of getting things across. Probably the most notable difference is that Mike Kelly used to work a lot with cones while Peter doesn't use them as much.

On a day to day basis, I'm training with Ben Roberts and Gary Walsh and maybe the youth team 'keepers, John Jackson and Chris Bennion. Gary has been in a difficult situation lately, losing his place in the team last season and then being completely out in the cold. Ben's been the one playing so far this season. He played in two cup finals last year and hasn't done anything wrong this season. But I've got complete confidence that the gaffer sees me as his number one. I'm not complacent about it because I know if I lose form there are other 'keepers who can take my place but I think I did well enough last season to deserve to get back in the side. It will be hard for Ben when I come back in and take his place but it happens to everyone when they're young.

You do notice a different feeling towards you from the other 'keepers but that's only natural. We all get on quite well but there is a rivalry there. I think it is impossible to be best friends at this level. But saying that, I've only once genuinely intensely disliked another 'keeper and that was at Kaiserslautern when I really would have wished him to have a nightmare. At that time, I was young, keen to learn and to get ahead, but this 37-year-old 'keeper took pleasure in making my life impossible.

The number one goalkeeper at the club was Andreas Reinke who was about 25 or 26 then and I got on with him very well but there was another goalkeeper, Gerhard Ehrman, who'd been at the club for about 12 years and he was loved by the crowd. He was nothing special but in training he used to kick the crap out of everyone, injure people and still everything was fine.

Most people in Germany are very arrogant but even more so in football. I think the reason for that is because there's a different structure to contracts in Germany. Players get paid a monthly allowance, about 50 per cent of the total package, another 30 per cent is dependent on appearances and 20 per cent is bonuses. So if you're playing you're earning more money but if you're not you're losing money. Everyone becomes an individual and there's always back-stabbing going on. The difference here is that when people aren't playing they're not annoyed because of the money, it's just because they want to play.

The money situation caused big problems for me at Kaiserslautern because you got a percentage of the appearance money if you sat on the bench. Ehrman must have had a contract where if he was sat on the bench he got 100 per cent of everything! He was supposed to be goalkeeping coach that season I was there but he pulled out and turned into a player again just to get his money. He made life very difficult for me and I asked to leave early because I couldn't get on the bench but they wouldn't let me go.

September 16th

Barnet 0 Boro 2
Coca-Cola Cup second round, second leg

I was a little bit nervous before the game at Barnet but no more than usual. Ben Roberts was on the bench as a precaution but I had no problems and it was a fairly comfortable comeback.

Barnet's a tight little ground and the crowd are really close to the pitch. It was a tricky surface and they could have made it hard for us, being only 1-0 up from the first leg. In the end we won quite easily with goals from Mikkel and Merse.

There were two more young lads making their debuts and they both did really well. Craig Harrison played left back and Steve Baker - who has to be the hairiest man in the world! - did very well at centre-back. If they keep going and get brought in gradually, I'm sure they'll both do well. It's difficult for the young lads when they're thrown in but they look very promising. A few weeks ago they were playing in the youth or reserve team. I don't know of any young player that will come in for 10 games and play consistently well for all of them. It's a big leap.

In Australia, there's a similar scheme to the YTS. At a young age you play in the schoolboy teams from under-sixes up. The club sides then play each other in the National Youth League where I was with Marconi from the age of 15. The youth team there was like a reserve team over here.

I came into the first team at 19. The next season I played 10 games and established myself to be the number one. I played three or four seasons there. In my first year we won the National League.

Merse spoke to the press after the game at Barnet and told them he was having problems coping with the travelling up to Teesside from his home in Hertfordshire every day. We've all had an idea that he has been finding it difficult.

It's maybe something that should have been kept within the club but Merse was promised something which he didn't get and was annoyed about it. He wanted to move into Ravanelli's house with his family, as had been agreed, but because Rav's transfer has dragged on so long he couldn't do it. His family have had to stay down south and he has been living in hotels which can't be easy. You also have to remember that Merse has never lived anywhere else but London, and Middlesbrough is very different to London.

Unfortunately, the stories are just going to add fuel to the fire and he will be linked with every club round London. The press seem to enjoy these kind of stories and see it as a chance to knock the local area.

It doesn't help for the image of the club and it gives people a chance to run Boro down. Once the press start hounding a club then they don't often let it go. There was a lot said before I was here when Emerson went AWOL last season and you don't want to give them any excuse.

There were definitely some people who enjoyed seeing Middlesbrough go down, having spent so much money and having brought in star foreigners. We have to get straight back to prove them wrong.

I have nothing against the Teesside area but I live with my girlfriend in Harrogate. I first met Paloma in Australia and met up with her again in Germany when she was travelling. We've been living together for two years now and plan to get married next summer, unless I'm playing in the World Cup. She's half-Spanish and that's another language I'm trying to learn. I would like to play in Spain some day. I love different cultures and I love hot weather.

Paloma works in Leeds as a commercial bank manager so Harrogate was a good place in between. I love the place. It's only 45 minutes away from Teesside but I like to be able to get away from the area. I can go out in Harrogate and not be bothered by anyone. Nobody wants to live in a goldfish bowl and, in a place that's as passionate about football as Middlesbrough, it would be difficult to get away from it. Even if I'm not playing well or the team's not playing well, I still want to go out for a meal or a drink with friends.

I've never had a problem with any Middlesbrough supporters but when I was in Germany I had people looking at me and saying: "How can you laugh?" when things weren't going well. Everybody needs to be able to relax and enjoy themselves even when things aren't going well at work.

It's a bit of a trek into Teesside from Harrogate but it's worth it. I sometimes travel in with Mikkel Beck who lives near Thirsk. When I arrived at the club, the first person I got talking to was Mikkel. I met him on the day I signed and Boro were playing against Newcastle. That's when I was introduced to everyone and he started speaking to me in German. Although Danish, he played in Germany with Fortuna Cologne before coming to Middlesbrough and he's fluent. He knew about me from my time in Germany and we've always spoken in German ever since. It's a good way for both of us to practice the language. I haven't always been fluent in German but, having spent two-and-a-half years there, I became fluent. I room with Mikkel on away trips. You tend to stick with the same people and have a routine. You have to find the right person to room with.

Although I get on well with the other players I'm not a big socialiser. I've had that experience before of going out drinking but the car accident taught me a lot and I don't tend to socialise that much with the other lads.

One of the things you miss when you're out injured is the dressing room atmosphere. There's always a joke or somebody getting stick for something or other.

The lads always seem to take the Mickey out of my black boots for some reason. I always get the Mickey taken out of my clothes. Merse has had a few digs at my haircut, calling me Wiggy, but he can hardly talk, with his flick.

I don't get as much stick for being an Aussie as I used to at Bradford. They used to call me a convict all the time which I had to dispute being only a second generation Aussie. The lads at Boro just call me Skippy.

There's some definite advantages to being an Aussie though and the Ashes has been one of them. It was a great chance to take the Mickey out of all the English lads. They should know better than to bet on England at cricket and I got £50 off Viv for England's predictable defeat.

The skipper, Nigel Pearson, is usually at the centre of things in the dressing room. He has a very dry sense of humour and is always the first one in with a comment and something to say. He's not as noisy as Viv though! He's definitely got the biggest mouth at the club.

When he's playing, Nigel has an unbelievable presence. He organises a lot and is excellent in the air. We're fortunate to have Nigel and Andy Townsend in the side as natural leaders. Even if Andy doesn't wear the armband, he always helps people out and shouts a lot. Andy's always at the centre of things and telling a story.

I've never known a dressing room with so many different languages. Gianluca Festa's English is pretty good and at least everybody appreciates that he's trying to learn. He's very funny and has a laugh with everyone. He'll have a go even if he gets it wrong and we all have a laugh about it.

Festa's good friends with Vlad Kinder and they're like twins - or is it Twins the movie, with Festa as the muscle-builder Arnold Schwarzenegger and Kinder as the short-arse, Danny De Vito!

Vlad doesn't seem to try so much with his English but maybe that's just a lack of confidence. Hopefully, when he learns more he'll come out of it. He's a very nice guy and understands the football talk on the pitch. Mind you, sometimes I yell out and he keeps running the other way so there must be a reason for that - or maybe it's just me!

Steve Vickers, Robbie Mustoe, Curtis Fleming and Derek Whyte are all close friends. Steve is fairly quiet but has a very dry sense of humour and comes out with snide remarks. It took me a while to get used to his sense of humour. Robbie is a lot of fun. You can take the Mickey out of him and he never takes it to heart. He's really good value.

Nigel, Andy Townsend and Merse get on well. They're the older lads who try and run things in the dressing room. Merse could whinge for England and he's only matched by Clayton Blackmore, who could whinge for Wales. Clayton has always got something to say which usually starts with "Can you believe it ..." Andy Townsend does a great impression of him complete with a Welsh accent.

Craig Hignett (Higgy) hangs around with different groups and goes off on his own. Emmo and Fabio generally go everywhere together but mix in as well sometimes. The funniest thing is that they look almost identical except that Fab is a Weightwatchers version! They have those 1970's perms, wear the same black shoes, stonewash jeans with no belt, 1986 polo shirt and mobile phones hooked on their jeans.

Then there's Phil Stamp, Alan Moore - who could whinge for Ireland! - and Craig Liddle. And the younger guys like Mark Summerbell, Ben Roberts, Anthony Ormerod, Andy Campbell and Craig Harrison hang around together.

Talking of Stampy, he's always got an excuse for not doing something. One time when he was late for treatment, he said it was because he had to take his dog to the vet and couldn't take it any other time because he hasn't got a car.

Stampy is the only footballer I know without a flash car. That's because he keeps failing his driving test. The last time he failed he was going towards a roundabout and the instructor said to go left. He was coming up behind a cyclist and left it too late to get in front of him. He wanted to cut the cyclist up and the instructor apparently almost jumped through the roof and told him to go straight on.

The funniest thing was that, on his previous test, he'd sworn at the instructor after he failed. Then, when he went back this time, it was the same guy!

The guys can't wait for him to come back from a test. He gets so nervous and we can't wait to get in to find out what went wrong. It must be three times he's failed now.

Ravanelli has finally left, signing for Olympique Marseille for £5.25 million. The club has had to cut its losses to some extent but it's still a decent amount of money. The longer it dragged on, the more chance there was that they could really struggle to off-load him.

Everybody is satisfied with the outcome. There's no denying that we're glad to get rid of him and there's a lot of relief that he has finally gone. He couldn't have come back from Italy again. There was no decision to be made because it had gone beyond that. It has dragged on for a long while and everyone's pleased. There have been a few jokes about having a party but mostly we're just pleased it is over. It was like a cloud hanging over the club.

I can honestly say that I've never met anyone like Ravanelli. In Germany, I was at clubs with top players like Andreas Brehme, the Czech internationals Pavel Kuka and Miroslav Kadlec, and Mikael Schjonberg, the Danish international. At Kaiserslautern, things didn't go at all well for Kuka but he still never put a foot out of line. Brehme is very arrogant and I don't like him as a person, but he's nothing like Ravanelli. He is still there for the team and would never behave in the way Rav has. It's already a better atmosphere at the club since he went back to Italy and that should continue now he's gone for good.

After hearing the news I travelled up to Newcastle to appear as a guest on the Tyne-Tees television programme, The Football Show. Inevitably, there were a few questions about Rav, and one of the hosts, Terry Christian, tried to have a few digs at the club. But it was an enjoyable night.

I've done other TV shows like Soccer AM on Sky and I did a few shows in Germany, though there it was harder with the cultural differences such as the different sense of humour. I do enjoy doing TV. It helps build your profile and get your personality across. I think there is a responsibility for players to do it because the supporters love to see it. It's part of the job.

One of the other guests was John Gorman, Glenn Hoddle's assistant at England. I had a chat with him and he seems a nice guy. I also met up again with the former Everton manager, Joe Royle, who was another one of the guests. When I left Bradford I had the choice of going to Everton or Middlesbrough and had a very bad experience at Goodison Park so it was interesting to see him again.

Joe didn't have too much to say to me but said some nice things on the show. He said I was among the top six 'keepers in the country. He didn't really mention what had happened at Everton except that they hadn't got their act together.

He got a lot of criticism last season because he tried to sign a few players and each time the player jumped to another club. I felt sorry for him because he seemed like a very nice guy but I've never met a chairman like Peter Johnson.

I wasn't in the negotiations but my agent Barry Silkman went in there and things didn't go anywhere near as well as we wanted. Everton seemed very cold. The chairman never seemed like he was interested in buying me even though they'd negotiated a fee with Bradford.

I turned up at Everton with my girlfriend Paloma and Barry. The chairman, as well as the vice-chairman and Joe Royle, were there. Peter Johnson's tone was very short and unfriendly from the start.

I sat down outside the office while my agent went in. The chairman asked if I wanted a coffee but I sat there and nothing happened. Then after about 20 minutes, Barry came out red-faced and said: "No deal, we're going." Joe Royle came out shaking his head and then the chairman came out smiling. He said something bizarre like: "Oh, you didn't get your coffee. Never mind, you won't be needing it now anyway." I heard later that that was the last straw. Joe Royle had a bit of a bust-up after that with the chairman and ended up leaving the club.

I went to speak to Middlesbrough afterwards. I found out later that Bryan Robson was really worried that I was going to do the same as Andrei Kanchelskis - go and see Everton and then Middlesbrough before going back to Everton to say: "This is what they've offered". But Barry said to Peter Johnson and also to me afterwards: "When we leave this building we are not coming back". Peter Johnson apparently replied: "Yeah, the doors open, come back any time". He was basically playing games, thinking that we would go back because it was Everton. He seemed to think that players would come just because it was Everton. He offered me ridiculously poor wages - I was almost earning the same amount at Bradford. But it wasn't just the money, I had a really bad feeling about the club.

Another reason I chose Middlesbrough over Everton was because Neville Southall was still there. I wasn't worried about removing him on the playing side but remembering the experience I had at Kaiserslautern with Geri Ehrman, I knew what it was like to have an old 'keeper around who had the crowd on his side. I feel sorry for the guy there now, Paul Gerrard.

Looking back now, even when Middlesbrough were relegated, I can honestly say that I've never regretted not joining Everton when I had the chance. I'm not enthralled about playing in the First Division but I have to see this as a short step back. I have to get back into the Premier League for my career and my international prospects. I've also got a taste of it and I want to be back there next year. I never thought about leaving Middlesbrough in the summer because I believe the club can get back there this season.

Ravanelli has sent a typical send off message by going to the News of the World having another go at the club and everyone. Whatever the right and wrong of what he's said, he's the only one who looks foolish. The Boro fans all know what he's like. They can see through what he's saying when he insists he gave 100 per cent in every game. They were very good to him when he finally came back considering what had happened.

When I left Kaiserslautern, I really felt hard done by with how I'd been treated. I seriously thought about going to the press and saying what I thought of several people but, at the end, it was pointed out to me that it would have been me that looked the idiot for whinging.

I know Rav was an emotional guy but it didn't help the way he had a go at other players on the pitch. There are players who get frustrated and show their feelings.

It was hard sometimes on Mikkel Beck who Rav tended to pick on most. Mikkel has a style sometimes when he doesn't look like he's giving everything but I know him well and I know he gives 100 per cent. The crowd get on his back sometimes and that doesn't help him.

With my return to action, the gaffer has allowed Gary Walsh to go on loan to my old club, Bradford. I actually mentioned Bradford to Gary because of my connections there. My agent also heard that they weren't happy with the 'keepers they had. I tried to ring Chris Kamara but he was away so I spoke to my agent and he said that if Gary was interested, he should give him a ring. He did, and the next day he had the choice of two clubs to join on loan.

It's been difficult for Gary. He was dropped last season and was then completely out of favour. It must have been on his mind that he was never going to get back in here. It didn't matter how well he played. He wanted to move back towards Lancashire particularly since his kids are starting school.

He has been pretty cool most of the time. There have been a couple of days when he was down but he picked himself up pretty quickly. It's not a good feeling. If you think you're training as good or better than the other 'keeper and still not getting a chance, it's a nightmare. I was in that situation at Kaiserslautern where I was training as well as the first choice and better than the second and still not getting a place on the bench.

I'm sure Gary will do well for Bradford because he is a good 'keeper. Chris Kamara knows a good player when he sees one (I should know!) and it may become a permanent move for Gary.

October 5th

Sunderland 1 Boro 2

A great win for my league return against the club's biggest rivals. They beat us 1-0 at home near the end of last season so it was a bit of revenge as well as being a local derby.

It was one of those games where I didn't really have a feeling which way it would go. They started well but we got on top in the second half and Emerson scored a great goal and set up the second. When he turns it on he's unbelievable. There's not many players that can do it like he does when he wants.

I didn't have much to do. Ben was still on the bench for precautionary reasons but the fitness has been coming back. I was a bit disappointed because I fell on my backside too early for their goal but that's probably just lack of match practice.

It was my first visit to Sunderland's new Stadium of Light and it's an unbelievable stadium. It makes a big difference to have it all closed in. There's empty corners at the Riverside and it's not the same. The atmosphere at Sunderland just ricochets off the walls. The crowd sounds like its 60 or 70 thousand not 40. It didn't feel like a First Division game.

My comeback came a bit too late to make Australia's squad for a friendly against Tunisia. We beat them 3-0 away which is a pretty good result because they've already qualified for the World Cup.

The first choice, Mark Bosnich, missed the game as expected because of Aston Villa's UEFA Cup game with Bordeaux and Zeljko Kalac played in goal. Portsmouth want to sign him but they're struggling to get a work permit because he hasn't played enough internationals. There's also the fact that he's had a permit previously and lost it because he didn't play enough games when he was at Leicester.

I'm hoping to get called up for the World Cup qualifier in November. It's a two-legged play-off to decide who gets to France. It looks like it might be the United Arab Emirates that we play.

chapter four

October

october 5th

Boro 1 Sheffield United 2

In the build-up to the game I was asked by the club's sponsors Cellnet to pose for a publicity picture. They had me dressed up as a Viking. I don't know why I get stuck with these things. I thought it was funny that they asked me to do it because Mikkel's the Scandinavian. The idea was that I was taking on Jan Fjortoft on his return to the club but he didn't even play! In the end, it was a bit of a non-event.

The game itself was a nightmare. We played quite well in the first half and took the lead but it was disappointing to concede a goal right after we'd scored. It was a silly goal, we were caught trying to play offside up on the half-way line. Brian Deane ran clean through one-on-one. I thought I should have saved it and Peter Shilton said the same to me afterwards. I always fancy my chances in one-on-ones even though the odds may be with the strikers and I was disappointed to be beaten.

There was a real drop in performance in the second half and we conceded another goal from a double flick-on. It's the second home defeat of the season already. We can't afford to drop many points at the Riverside if we want to get promoted. We were all down because we couldn't believe how poorly we had played in the second half.

It was disappointing for me because it's only the second game I've lost at the Riverside. The other was against Stockport in the Coca-Cola Cup semi-final but even then it wasn't really a defeat because we qualified for the final.

Before the game, Paul Merson heard that he'd been recalled by England for the vital qualifying game against Italy. It's fully deserved because he's been excellent since he joined us. You can see that he's really excited about it. He's had a few worries about moving up to Middlesbrough but this must be a boost to his confidence. He's been linked with a lot of other clubs after talking about his travelling but he's committed himself to the club and he's been playing really well. He's very important to our promotion hopes.

It's been very quiet around the club with a lot of the players away on international duty. Merson has gone to join the England squad for the World Cup decider against Italy and we've got a lot of internationals at the club.

There's always something to do and you just have to get on with it. Training is a bit dull but you have to concentrate on your own fitness. We were all given the weekend off with so many players being away on international duty and having no game ourselves. I went away to the Yorkshire Dales for a few days. We didn't have cable in the place we were staying so I watched the replay of the England game later on and we managed to avoid hearing the score. I thought they played really well and deserved to go through to the finals, drawing 0-0.

Luca Festa was very confident before the game. There have been all sorts of bets going on and Festa's going to have to pay out some big money. When he came in after the game he kept his head very low and didn't say much until everyone took the Mickey out of him and he was fine. I didn't have a bet with him because, to be honest, I would have backed Italy - though I didn't tell any of the boys that!

Australia's next international isn't until next month. I'm hoping to be back in the squad. I've got five caps for my country now and I obviously want more.

My debut was back in 1993 in a game in Canada. It was a World Cup qualifying play-off over two legs in the lead-up to the 1994 USA World Cup and it was the time when Mark Bosnich decided he didn't want to play because he didn't want to miss games for Aston Villa. He pulled out at the last minute and was then suspended for the rest of the World Cup qualifiers by the Australian Federation.

I was called in as the second 'keeper. I had been away on holiday in Germany for six weeks. For the first two weeks I'd been training with Bayer Leverkusen. This was a year before I joined Dresden and I was seeing what it was like. But I hadn't trained for four weeks when I was called up. I had a couple of weeks in the gym and then a week in the build-up to the game but I was on the bench so I wasn't too worried about my lack of fitness.

But then 16 minutes into the game the 'keeper Robert Zabica came out of his box and committed a foul. I thought he would just get booked but then the ref showed him the red card. It suddenly dawned on me that I would be going on. I was only 20 and hadn't thought that I would be playing. The coach, Eddie Thomson, turned to me and told me to get my gear off. Soon after, we took the lead but lost 2-1. I couldn't do anything about the goals and I was quite happy about the way I played.

Two weeks later it was the return leg back in Sydney. There was a lot of discussion about whether I would play. Bosnich was still suspended. There was talk of him coming back but then he announced he was retiring from international football completely. Zabica was suspended and in the end I was given the chance. We won the game 2-1. I was disappointed with the goal we conceded but we won 4-1 on penalties and I saved two.

We were then through to play Argentina over two legs to see who would go to the finals. The first game was in Australia and there was a lot of hype because it was Diego Maradona's first game back after coming out of retirement. Suddenly Mark Bosnich decided he wanted to play again and all the talk about him being suspended or retired was forgotten. Zabica had also served his suspension so he was on the bench and I was sat in the stands. We drew the game 1-1. We played well and they only had one chance where Gabriel Batistuta scored an unbelievable header. We had a goal disallowed and really should have won the game comfortably.

Our bad luck continued in the second leg away in Argentina. Bosnich decided he didn't want to play again. He said he was injured so he stayed in England. The coach decided to play Zabica and I was on the bench. Argentina won 1-0 with a very lucky goal. It was a cross from almost on the goal-line and it deflected off a defender, looped over the 'keeper, hit the far post and went in. That was our chance of reaching the finals gone.

My next game was in a friendly international against South Africa a couple of months later. It was their first away international in something like 30 years. We played them twice and I was supposed to be on the bench for the first game and start the second. I ended up coming on in the first because the other 'keeper, Zeljko Kalac, broke his collarbone with 15 minutes to go. We won both games. Since then the only time I have played was for 15 minutes in a friendly against Saudi Arabia. Hopefully, there will be more to come.

october 15th

Boro 2 Sunderland 0
Coca-Cola Cup third round

Some of the young lads came back in for the Coca-Cola game against our local rivals and again did really well. Andy Campbell scored the first goal and we tied it up with a late strike from Craig Hignett.

A few people have said it devalues the competition to play youngsters but, especially against teams like Barnet in the last round, I don't see anything wrong with it. We are still playing a strong balanced side and the gaffer has usually played experienced players through the middle of the team. If the kids can't do it against a Third Division team like Barnet then they're not going to be good enough. They played well then and deserved their chance to show what they could do in a bigger game.

It was one of the quietest games I've ever had. There was only one shot to save. Apart from that it was only corners and crosses that I had to deal with. Some 'keepers say they like having quiet games and not being involved. It's a Catch 22, if you're working hard then the team's not doing well but I like being involved and helping win games. You have to concentrate hard in the game so you don't make the one mistake that costs your team victory. There was one back pass that I miscontrolled which caused a few missed heartbeats but I always thought I would get to it.

When I first started playing, kicking wasn't such a big part of the game but it's something you get used to. I used to play out of goal in five-a-sides a lot in Germany and it helps you adapt to controlling and kicking the ball. I enjoy playing out on field in training.

In the dressing room the next day, we heard about some trouble after the game. The story is that some Boro fans threw stuff at the Sunderland team coach but there were some stories going round that it was Sunderland supporters who were unhappy with their team. Whoever it was you don't want to see that sort of thing in football. It does sour the occasion.

The only experience I have had like that was a strange one when I went to play in an under-20 World Cup qualifier, in Fiji of all places. A little kid ran up and threw a brick at the window of the bus. The bus had bars across all the windows so they were obviously used to that kind of violence! Players do notice a better atmosphere now. There's more families and football stadia are less hostile places.

oCtober 18th

Crewe 1 Boro 1

We almost never made it to Crewe. We were at Teesside airport on the morning of the game and there was thick fog. The plane tried to land twice but couldn't and was running out of fuel so it had to go back to Newcastle. It then came back and we were all sat in our cars ready to drive down to Crewe when it finally landed at the second attempt.

It was another nightmare game. It was one of those days when it had been freezing cold for weeks and then it was normal. I'm saying normal but there are no normal days in England. It was about 20 degrees and full sunshine.

The whole team and coaching staff struggled. They were a bunch of kids, no disrespect, and we should have taken them apart. Their equaliser from Dele Adebola was a great goal but I'm not sure he meant to put it right where it went. I had no chance but, to be honest, I thought it was going wide.

The whole team and coaching staff had a heated discussion a couple of days after the game in the canteen at the training ground. We talked about the attitude of everyone. We're not demanding enough of each other and pulling our own weight. There's probably not enough people pushing each other along. It may have something to do with the Ravanelli thing. Some players might be frightened that one of the big name players will turn round and say "who the hell are you?" but we need to work as a team.

october list

Oxford 1 Boro 4

We met up again with former team-mate Phil Whelan before the game. He left the club to go to Oxford in the summer. It wasn't until I saw him sat in the dug-out with his foot in plaster that I realised he'd broken his leg. I never actually played with Phil but he was always a nice guy and I have a lot of sympathy for him because he's done the same injury as I had.

Just before the game we were in the dressing room when we saw smoke coming from the toilets. Then Emmo came out laughing - he'd been smoking in there. All the gaffer could do was shake his head and laugh. But Emmo still went out and scored the first goal to put us 1-0 up at half-time.

Five minutes into the second half they scored from a corner which made us a bit nervous but we came back quickly. It must have been some game because Robbie Mustoe scored with a header (we think it was probably his nose) and Curtis got one as well.

october 25th

Boro 2 Port Vale 1

The team has picked up quite a few injuries and the young lads are having to come into the side. The experience of playing in the Coca-Cola Cup will be good for them and no-one has let the team down yet. Craig Harrison and Steve Baker came in for their league debuts and another youngster, Kris Trevor, was on the bench. Derek Whyte also made his first league start. He's had the chance to move to Tranmere but felt it wasn't right for him. It's incredible that, apparently, 26 different players have been involved in the first team already and it's only October.

We were a bit lucky to beat Port Vale. Merse scored both our goals from the penalty spot. I didn't get a clear view of either, being down the other end of the pitch, but everyone says the first was a definite penalty while the second was controversial. It wasn't a convincing performance but we probably just about deserved to win. We were hanging on a bit at the end and I had to make a couple of saves before they pulled one back in the last minute. Robbie Mustoe had to go off in the first half and we look as if we will have a lot of experienced players out for the game against Huddersfield on Tuesday.

october 28th

Boro 3 Huddersfield 0

It was a great result considering the players we had playing. We finished the game with three teenagers in the back five and another making his first team debut. We were really struggling to put a side out and it shows there's good depth in the squad.

The player making his debut was Emerson's cousin Fabio. He surprised everyone. I'd never seen him play before so it was a bit of an eye-opener. Some of the boys had told me before that they thought he was a good player but nobody expected him to do so well. He's played quite a bit in the reserves but no-one was sure he could make the step up.

Huddersfield hadn't won a game all season and it was very important that we beat them. We dominated the game and won comfortably 3-0. It's nice to get a clean sheet for a change. Mikkel got two goals and Merse the other. Their partnership seems to have worked really well. I think Merse is playing a little bit out of position but he's scoring goals for fun at the moment - four in three games. We're starting to get into a winning rhythm now and this result takes us into the top three for the first time.

I don't generally read the papers but I hear from the boys that they're saying that Ravanelli has taken everything out of the club house he lived in that wasn't nailed or glued down. Merse is moving in there so he won't be too impressed. Obviously Rav wasn't very happy with the situation when he was leaving. Some people react differently to situations of anger and I guess he showed his true colours.

chapter five

November

november 1st

Wolves 1 Boro 0

We really should have got a point. Wolves played out of their skin and I don't think they'll play like that again all season, except maybe when we play them again! The goal we conceded was late on when we should have been able to hang on for a point. They'd never really looked like scoring despite dominating the game. The chance came from nothing and young Robbie Keane, who looks like he's going to be some player, hit it over me.

We are conceding too many late goals. We lack a bit of concentration. Instead of thinking "there's 15 minutes to go, we should hold on to the lead", we tend to keep pressing and trying to score an extra goal. We've hardly conceded a goal in the first half all season. As a 'keeper I pride myself on clean sheets and we haven't been getting them. We're only conceding one goal in most games but we can't hang on to things at the moment.

We are definitely missing a striker. I don't think Merse is an out-and-out striker. The gaffer knows it and is looking for someone. At the moment, especially at home when teams are packing their defence, we're struggling with only one or one-and-a-half players up front as Merse is dropping back a lot of the time to try and create things. With only one man up front it needs to be a great ball to reach him.

Neil Maddison came in for his debut in a difficult game and did well in the sweeper/central defensive position. He signed from Southampton just a few days before the game. He's very versatile and can also play in midfield or full-back apparently. It's useful to have players who can slot into a few different positions.

Emerson keeps getting linked with moves away every week. He did an interview with Sky that was picked up by all the papers, saying he was leaving. He says to us that he's going each week but it's a bit of a joke. I think all the papers are a bit annoyed that he doesn't give any interviews and they took the chance to use it. Emmo says it was all taken out of context which wouldn't surprise me.

As long as he's still here and playing well there's no problem. We all know what happened last season and you're never quite sure what Emmo's going to get up to. He might decide to leave at some point but there's no point worrying about it.

Gary Walsh has signed permanently for Bradford. He's done very well on loan there. It was a much needed move for him and he was dying to get out. It would have been cruel for him to have had to come back and not play. He was completely out of the gaffer's plans and needed a fresh start.

His kids are just starting school and he can now move back to Manchester and get his family situation settled. From my experience of being there, I could only recommend Bradford to him. They've got a decent side together and Chris Kamara has made them hard to beat. They've got off to a good start and I always thought they would do well this year.

Meanwhile, Ben Roberts has been picked for the England under-21 squad for their game next week. It's good news for him after what's been a frustrating time since losing his place in the side. He's only young and he should have a good future ahead of him. The England set-up clearly rate him and the manager here has had no problem with playing him whenever he's needed to. It's hard when you're a young 'keeper and you are dropped as soon as the number one comes back but all 'keepers go through it in their younger days and he has to bide his time.

One of the biggest issues at the moment is betting on matches. The FA are trying to crack down because there's question marks about match-fixing and so on. In my experience, footballers always bet on matches. Our lads bet on Premier League and European games and stuff but not on our own division. I tend to just bet on the cricket and rugby because when it's Australia they're certainties!

There's obviously a danger when people are betting on the time of the first throw-in or whatever and then you get into the area of match-fixing. I can honestly say that I've never come across it and I can't understand how anyone could do it.

Another big story is the case of the ex-footballer Ian Knight who is in the courts trying to get compensation for a tackle that wrecked his career. It's a very delicate situation because if a player injures you in a tackle and ruins your career, it's only natural to be bitter and want to get something out of it. In the Ian Knight case, I've seen the tackle on TV and the footage isn't great but it doesn't look like much. I've seen worse tackles and the one which injured Denis Irwin in Manchester United's Champions League game against Feyenoord looked nasty.

There are too many bad tackles going on in the game. Players get away with a lot. When I broke my leg, it was from a tackle that could have ended my career, although it didn't look bad. I would certainly have had to think about whether to pursue it legally.

Players don't tend to talk about it much because people are nervous about it, thinking it might bring bad luck. One minute you could be running round the pitch fine and the next you could be on the end of a nasty tackle and never play again. It's a very fine line.

Craig Hignett's been getting a bit of stick from the lads because his wife went on the local radio station phone-in. She said he was always the scapegoat if we didn't play well. Higgy's had heaps of stick for that and then his wife was in The Sun the next day talking about being a footballer's wife. He's not going to live that down for a while.

November 5th

Boro 1 Portsmouth 1

Another player getting a bit of stick is Craig Harrison. He does modelling in his spare time and has been in magazines and newspapers. Then he was on the cover of today's programme looking like a model so he got some stick for that. It's all in good humour. The young kids are very level-headed and quiet. A lot of the older lads have taken to them.

We went ahead in the game when Andy Townsend sneaked in at the back post after Merse had played the ball in. We really should have gone on to win the game against a side struggling at the bottom of the table but we threw it away. One through ball caught out the defence and their guy finished the one-on-one.

Like I said the other week, we need to learn when we get in front not to let teams get back at us. Quite a few of the lads had words to say afterwards. It was a stupid way to lose two points. We should have been consolidating when we were ahead rather than going for more goals. We left gaps at the back and paid the price. It was an incredibly disappointing result and we had more than enough chances to win two games.

The gaffer wasn't at the game. We never get told too much but apparently he's been out in Italy trying to sign the striker Michele Padovano from Juventus. I don't know much about him but we could certainly do with strengthening in that department.

Terry Venables wasn't at the game. He was apparently commentating on a European game instead. I don't think he's seen me play for a long time and that's disappointing with the squad about to be announced for the World Cup play-off games. There were several other Aussies in the game with the Portsmouth connection but I only know two of them - John Aloisi and Craig Foster. They were both very quiet on the night. John is potentially a very good player, sharp around the box and scores goals. Craig is a bit older so I'm not sure whether he'll do that well.

My fears have been proved right after hearing the Australian squad. It's no surprise to see all the Portsmouth players there. No-one from the international set-up bothered to tell me I hadn't been selected and I heard from a newspaper guy. I don't know whether anyone's been to see me play but we've been on Sky a few times so they've had opportunities. I'm very disappointed but not surprised.

I had a feeling it was coming. The assistant coach, Raul Blanco, was quoted saying that it was unlikely I would be picked as I hadn't played enough games. When I actually saw who they had picked, this reason seemed ridiculous. The second 'keeper, Zeljko Kalac, has played two games in six months while Portsmouth are trying to sign him. The third choice - Jason Petkovic - plays back in Australia and no-one knows who he is. The league over there is maybe equivalent to the Second or Third Division here.

I do feel insulted. There are four or five players in the squad who have played less games than me but apparently that's the reason I haven't been picked. I've played 11 games and the second and third 'keeper have played six or seven between them.

Mark Bosnich is, of course, the first choice. No one can argue with that but looking back to the Stockport game last year it seems there's one rule for some and another for others. I get dropped for pulling out of a game and Bozza pulled out for a UEFA Cup game but Venables turns round and says he wasn't going to play him anyway.

I've given a bit of a whinge in the papers back home. It's something I know I shouldn't have done. I said I thought Terry Venables was favouring his players from Portsmouth and that I'd had enough and didn't care about the national team anymore. John Aloisi is a good player but I think the others are just in the squad because of the club they play for. I also believe that Kalac is only in the squad as number two, where he will be on the bench and has a chance of coming on, because they are trying to get a work permit for him to join Portsmouth.

Saying what I said won't do me any favours but it's been a frustrating time for me. I thought I'd fought back from the injury quickly enough to be considered and was playing well enough to deserve to be involved. Everyone else is thinking the same thing so I decided to be the one who said it publicly. You get frustrated and it got it off my chest.

November 8th

Boro 3 QPR 0

We played tremendously well and they hardly had a chance. They were very poor. Becky and Merson got another goal each and we ran riot. Anthony Ormerod came on and got another near the end. He then did a spectacular somersault flip. It's quite impressive if you get it right but I won't be trying it.

The deal for Michele Padovano has all fallen through. Apparently his agent asked for too much money and he's going to Crystal Palace. I don't know anything about this agent but there are a lot of very dodgy ones around.

I had a bad experience with one in Germany. When I moved from Bradford to Middlesbrough he thought he was entitled to a cut even though he had nothing to do with the deal and our contract was no longer valid. He sent me a huge bill. He still had my tax returns as well as two budgies of mine - and he held them to ransom! I had to contact my solicitor to get the documents back. We had to threaten to take him to court and eventually I got the budgies as well!

It's a strange decision by Padovano to go to Palace when you compare our relative positions. They're in the Premier League but struggling. I hadn't heard of him but Festa said he's OK. I think a lot of the players are relieved because we didn't fancy another Italian. Rav definitely left a sour taste in our mouths.

The reception to my comments in the press has been quite good. I've heard nothing whatsoever from Terry Venables, not even in the press, but nearly everyone else has been positive. It's been very big news in the media back in Oz. Every soccer show on TV has focused on it. At least there's no danger of people forgetting about me over there now.

A few Australian internationals have come out and backed what I have said. One, Frank Farina, who's very well respected, said he agreed with me. Quite a few people have jumped on the bandwagon and had a go at Terry Venables. A few people have accused me of whinging but most appreciate that it's not just sour grapes.

One of the people who hasn't taken too kindly to my comments is Zeljko Kalac. He's accused me of stabbing him and the other players in the back but I can't see that. I've known him since we were in the national under-12 squads together and I've nothing against him. I was criticising Venables and pushing my own cause, not having a go at Kalac. The press just turned it round so it seemed that way.

The simple fact is that I was left out because I supposedly haven't played enough games. But some of the others had played four or five games in a few months back in Australia at a standard that's maybe the equivalent of the English Third Division. I've played 11 games now and I'll have played a few more by the time the game comes around. I believe I deserve to be in the squad ahead of them and can't understand why I wasn't.

No-one from the Australian Federation has said anything. I'm sure a few people agree with me but they want to qualify for the World Cup at all costs. Rightly or wrongly, they believe Terry Venables is the right man and they're prepared to overlook any criticism. The thing is that it's pretty much common knowledge that he won't be there much longer. I've heard from very good sources that he's moving to another coaching position even if we do qualify.

Bryan Robson has come out and said I should be in the squad. It's nice to hear and his comments have been reported back in Australia as well. He did say to me that he thought I shouldn't have said anything to the press because it would jeopardise my chances of getting to the World Cup but this has been going on too long and somebody really needed to say something. I probably have blown it but, with the way things were going, I didn't think I was going to get a look in anyway so I really had nothing to lose.

The game is a two-legged match against a team from Asia. I do think that FIFA are making it very hard for Australia to qualify. Last time out we had to win our qualifying competition then beat Canada, who finished second in the CONCACAF region, and then the best placed team that had missed out from South America which was Argentina. The problem is that we are miles ahead of all the other Oceania teams. Some of the games are embarrassing. We beat the Solomon Islands 13-0 in one game. There is no way we are ever going to not win the group.

The team we will be playing is Iran. While we have won all our games, they failed to qualify from their group but still got another chance with a play-off against Japan. They lost that but still get another chance. They've had three chances but we have only one. I think we should go into the Asian qualifying group. Maybe the Oceania qualifying could start earlier and once we have got through that we could go into a group with some of the Asian countries. At least then we would have a fair chance.

november 15th

Norwich 1 Boro 3

Norwich are a really difficult team to play away from home and I remember losing 2-0 there with Bradford last season. I had loads to do that day. We went 1-0 down today when big Iwan Roberts scored a really good header. We pulled one back just before half-time and came out and got two good goals on the break afterwards. Norwich haven't been doing too well but it's still a really good result.

Merse was due to miss the game because he was in the England squad but the gaffer asked for him to be released as he wasn't going to play and he played for us instead. We've still got a few injuries and we needed him to play. Anthony Ormerod also started when he was expected to miss the game. Him and Andy Campbell were in the England under-18 squad the night before in Crewe but didn't play so they came down in the middle of the night and joined us at the hotel. Anthony played well and got another goal. He's looking really promising.

november 18th

Boro 2 Bolton 1
Coca-Cola Cup third round

It just goes to show that we can match it with the Premier League teams. We should have won the game before extra-time because we had enough chances even before they had a man sent off for two bookings in the second half. They scored first and it took a bit of wind out of our sails. The goal came from nothing. They took a short corner and it came across to Alan Thompson. He had a shot blocked but the rebound fell to him and as I was getting back up, it came through a crowd of players and into the net.

We bounced back and Mark Summerbell scored the equaliser soon after. He looks to be an exceptional young player. He's strong and aggressive despite not being the biggest and he looks to be a good footballer as well. He could have scored another one in the second half but it took until extra-time when Higgy put the ball away.

Our reward for beating Bolton is a quarter-final tie with Reading. It's away and obviously we'd prefer to be at home but we've avoided the big teams and we couldn't have asked for much more. I wouldn't be frightened of anyone but this does give us a great chance of getting into the semis. With that being two legs, we've got to fancy our chances of going all the way back to Wembley.

My brother, Daniel, has arrived for a few months over from Australia. Like me, he's a goalkeeper and has come over to have a few trials in England. He's 15 so he might be a bit young but he wants to see what it is like in England.

Daniel plays for a team called Southern Districts in Sydney. My old club Marconi has its own junior set-up but it has also taken over the youth side of another club, Southern Districts, who play at the same ground. They couldn't afford their juniors anymore so Marconi took it over. Southern Districts still has a separate first and reserve team but my brother is to all intents and purposes a Marconi player and would join Marconi if he does well.

Marconi are a semi-professional club. At the time I was there, and for about 10 years before, it was probably the top club in the country. It's a heavily supported Italian club, hence the name Marconi after the wireless inventor, and a huge club. Football clubs in Australia are very different to England. The stadiums are much smaller and the clubs are licensed clubs that have poker machines, cards, betting, bars, discos, function rooms and are open all day like a leisure club. It has something like 15,000 members.

The club itself has expanded immensely in the past few years but the football side has suffered a bit. When I was there, they won the championship two years in a row. The third year, we lost in the final. The next year we finished seventh or eighth. I came into the side for the last 10 games of that season and we won the league again the next year in my first full season. After that we finished third but a lot of players left following that season.

The club has produced quite a few good players that have moved on to do well in Europe. Steve Corica came over to England to join Leicester City then moving on to join Wolves. He's had a lot of injury problems recently but has done quite well. Frank Farina went on to play for Club Bruges in Belgium, Bari in Italy and Strasbourg. Paul Okon was also at Bruges and is now at Lazio. Mark Bosnich also started at Marconi before going on to Manchester United as an apprentice and then to Aston Villa.

Another player I played with at youth level was Christian Vieri who now plays for Atletico Madrid and Italy. His father played for Juventus and Italy but married an Australian woman and went out to Australia. Vieri was very good as a youngster but went to Italy when he was about 15. I can still remember the day when we had a game and he didn't turn up. The bus went round to his house, which was just around the corner from the ground, and his dad said that he wouldn't be playing any more.

Daniel is quite highly rated over there and is hoping to follow in my footsteps. I think it would do him good to play in Australia for a while longer but it should be good experience for him to come over here. I haven't seen much of him for a few years since I came to Europe so it should be good for us.

The recent rugby league series between Australia and England has led to a few bets with a couple of the local media men, Gordon Cox and Alastair Brownlee. I cleaned up on the First Test. I gave Coxy a 15 point start and we sailed home by 24. Alastair was even easier to beat as we started from scratch.

I thought my luck was in when we didn't bet on the second test when England won. They were gutted and were very keen to bet on the third.

This time I was sure we were going to cruise it and sure enough we went 28 points up in the game. We'd bartered our way to a 19 point start in the betting and I thought I'd be laughing all the way to the bank. But then England scored to pull it back to a 23 point lead. And then in the last 20 seconds, England scored again, right in the corner. The 19 point lead was just still on though until they managed an impossible kick from the touchline. To everyone else it was just consolation and England had still been stuffed. All the Aussie players were celebrating but I couldn't join them as I was £40 down from these two. Even Ben Roberts had taken me for a tenner.

Australia have drawn 1-1 away in Iran in the first leg of the World Cup play-off. Harry Kewell, of Leeds, scored the goal and apparently Mark Bosnich played very well in goal. With the second leg at home we should be very confident of getting through. Not being involved does have its advantages for me because rather than sitting on the bench in Iran, I'm here playing games for Middlesbrough.

november 22nd

Swindon 1 Boro 2

Swindon hadn't lost at home all season but we went there and won 2-1 - a great result. It's the first of three games against the sides above us in the table and a great start. They scored first - yet again. George Ndah, making his debut, played a one-two and put it past me as I tried to narrow the angles.

I always worry when we go behind but this season we seem to be able to come back. Last season we never did that. There is definitely a lot more togetherness in the squad and everyone fights for each other. That seems to be working for us on the pitch.

We equalised when Mikkel closed the 'keeper down and his clearance fell to Merse. He just knocked it back in to the goal. You feel for 'keepers in that situation but he had plenty of time to get rid of it and maybe it was just rustiness as he had been out for a while injured before the game.

The winner came from the unlikely source of Emerson's head. It's almost unheard of for that to happen but, mind you, he could hardly miss. It was right on the line.

november 26th

Boro 0 Nottingham Forest 0

We played very well against the league leaders and were unlucky not to win. In the first half we were nearly made to pay for a couple of sloppy defensive headers but they didn't create too much and in the second half we put them under pressure and should have won.

Emerson should have scored when he was one-on-one in the first half and there were a couple Dave Beasant parried that we couldn't quite get on the end of. Beasant had a tremendous game. He made a couple of excellent saves. I've always thought he's quite a good 'keeper but he is prone to the odd howler. He seems to have bad games when teams really can't afford it and gets all the headlines. That happens when you're a 'keeper and it's something you have to come to terms with. It's like Fraser Digby at Swindon in the last game. You can have loads of solid games and then make one mistake and you're remembered for that. David James is another one. He was outstanding at the start of last season and got into the England squad. Then he makes a few mistakes and people forget the good things. Unfortunately, Liverpool were desperate for the title and his errors were a good excuse for missing out.

november 29th

Boro 1 West Brom 0

There was some doubt as to whether I would play as I picked up a virus that has been doing the rounds at the club. I was heaving and felt light-headed on Thursday night and on the Friday morning I rang Bob Ward to tell him. He advised me to stay at home and stay in bed. Fortunately, on the morning of the game I felt better. I was still light-headed and a bit under the weather but I was well enough to play. Nigel Pearson though had to miss the game.

Mind you, after seeing Australia play against Iran this morning, I felt considerably worse. I switched on after 20 minutes and it was goalless. Apparently, in the first few minutes we should have had four or five but even when I watched we looked the better side. We finally took our chances and with 15 minutes to go we were 2-0 up and cruising. We should have walked it but I still had a feeling that we weren't as comfortable as we should have been. Then it all fell apart. Iran scored twice in a few minutes and we were out.

On that performance we didn't deserve to go through. On the chances we had we should have walked it but the defending was atrocious and we gifted them the game. Once the first goal went in we were all over the place. I felt a bit sorry for Bosnich because he had nothing to do all game and he had no chance with the goals.

It was so disappointing because there were 95,000 people in the stadium and football has been getting the most attention it ever has in Australia. If we had qualified it would have been a big boost for the game there. If I'm honest, in some ways, I'm glad because it might bring about changes. But I'm an Australian and I would love to see my country at the World Cup. We really should have been there and questions have got to be asked.

I also hadn't given up hope of getting there myself, with a change of heart - or manager! It's now more than four years until the next World Cup. There's nothing like the European Championships to look forward to so I've lost a major chance to take part in a World Cup. There aren't many chances and you can see why I was so disappointed to be overlooked. I will be 28 when the next World Cup comes around and, although I will hopefully have a couple more chances, it is a big blow.

I wasn't expecting to play. I know Mark Bosnich is the first choice and I can't argue with that. He's playing in the Premier League and is the man with the jersey now. But I would expect to be number two. And being there, you never know what could have happened. Middlesbrough could win promotion and I could get the attention, Bosnich could have lost form or got injured. Anything could have happened.

Australia have now got a tournament in Saudi Arabia to look forward to. It will be a nightmare for the players because it is the last thing they will want to do. I'm glad I'm not there now because I would be missing games for Middlesbrough taking part in a pointless tournament. Managers who are losing players for it must be very annoyed. They'll have lost players for about four weeks, like Harry Kewell at Leeds and Stan Lazaridis at West Ham.

It's very difficult when you're an Australian international, playing your club football on the other side of the world. When the Irish lads at Boro get called up they can play on a Wednesday and be back at the club the next day. I would need four or five days to get out to Australia and get over the jet lag and the same to come back. You need about 10 days for each game.

At least Middlesbrough managed to win our game against WBA. It's two clean sheets in a row for the first time this season but this time we sneaked a goal as well and came away with the three points. We didn't play that well but the good thing was that we still won.

The club's former 'keeper Alan Miller played very well for West Brom on his return to the Riverside and made a couple of excellent saves. He left just as I was arriving at the club so I don't know him really but he's been a big part of the success at West Brom this season. They did play very well in the first half and created a few chances but they didn't get any on target. The funny thing is that even when we have lost games this season I've never had much to do. There hasn't been a game yet where I've come off thinking I've been really busy.

Mikkel scored our goal and had a great game. He's been playing really well recently and his game seems to have picked up. After the cup game against Bolton, when he played well, the gaffer said he wanted him to play like that all the time and he's responded to that. The crowd were chanting his name and that was great to hear. He's got a lot of stick from them and it's got to be good for his confidence. I know Mikkel and he's always tried to do his best but now he's adapting his game more to the English style. It's never easy when the crowd's on your back. Wherever you go there are always players that fans have a go at. In Germany, I think it's probably worse and they're even harder on players.

chapter six

December

A new player has arrived at the club and it's a familiar one for many of the lads. Jaime Moreno spent two years at the club before going to America to play for Washington. I don't know him but the lads say he's quite a character. He's a Bolivian international and looks quite sharp in training. He'll provide extra cover for the striking positions. He's done quite well in the US but, judging from what I've seen on TV, the standard's not too good so it will be interesting to see if he can adapt.

december 2nd

Ipswich 1 Boro 1

Another game thrown away with a late goal. We played well and were very unlucky to have Craig Harrison sent off. Craig was elbowed by their striker James Scowcroft and he then punched Craig. I don't think Craig did anything wrong. It was a farce because the referee first sent off Andy Townsend and then changed his mind and sent off Craig. I've never seen anything like it.

It was difficult conditions because there had been snow and the pitch was icy. But anyway, we should have won. They scored late on and within a minute the whistle had gone for full time. The goal came from a cross which was headed down towards the goal. Their guy got a flick on, I went for it, missed it, it hit the post, bounced back off the post, and they hit it in before I got up again. We should have won the game easily as we had three or four one-on-ones. It was a long day and we didn't get back until about 3.00 am.

There's a story in the papers that Juninho is unhappy in Spain and might be coming back to Middlesbrough. We asked Emmo, who's in contact with Juninho, and he said he wasn't unhappy. He likes Spain. He doesn't get on that well with some of the players but you get that at big clubs.

I can't see him coming back but if he did, there wouldn't be any bad feeling just because he left when we were relegated. If we were to get into the Premier League, there is no doubt we would buy new players. There might be some players annoyed to lose their position but that could happen whoever came in.

december 6th

Bury 0 Boro 1

Before the game we would have been happy to come away with a draw because they are such a difficult team to play against. They are a big, strong team and they play high balls up to the front. The conditions were difficult as well. We didn't play that well but we did enough to win the game which was the important thing. They had one or two chances in the first half but we deserved to win. Becky got another goal and he and Merse have now both reached double figures.

Straight after the Bury game, the whole team went away together for a trip to Dublin. It was an ideal time to go. There was a great feeling because we'd just gone top of the league. It's the first time I've been away with the lads and it turned out to be a very long weekend.

When we arrived on the Saturday night, we went to a bar, then a disco before everyone went their separate ways. Viv and I came out of a night-club late that night and tried to get a cab. There was a queue of about 20 people and we would have had to wait an hour for a taxi. Then this guy came up in a bicycle rickshaw. I couldn't believe it because it was freezing cold. As we were going along, we realised this guy was going the wrong way. We told him but he said that this was the only way to go without going uphill. Even so, he was knackered by the time we got to the hotel and Viv agreed a tenner as the fee which I hotly disputed. I got in quite early that night ... at 3.30 am.

It was lunch-time before I got up on the Sunday but some of the lads were already in the bar. It started all over again. It was a great day with everyone together and having a good time. The locals reacted really well to us. Andy

Townsend was in his element and Curtis Fleming seemed to know every man and his dog. Coming from the city, he certainly knew every bar owner in Dublin and they all gave us a good time. There was plenty of alcohol consumed but it was great for team spirit and this sort of thing really helps morale. There was plenty of jokes and carrying-on and that brings you closer together.

Mark Summerbell earned a new nickname, "Vice-Captain Booze", for his exploits. He surprised everyone with his ability to hold his drink. Emmo, Nigel and Flem weren't bad on the drinking side either. Summers and I were probably the last home most nights. One night, we were walking home and he went to kick a garbage bag and there was nothing in it. He slipped and ended up on his backside. That would have taken some explaining to the gaffer if he had been injured.

Two of the other young lads weren't allowed to go - Anthony Ormerod and Andy Campbell. "Dad" John Pickering, our first team coach, put his foot down and made them stay at home. John didn't behave too well himself and ended up in a garden one night. He had one or two too many and fell into a garden on his way home from a pub across the road from the hotel.

Alan Moore had a scare as well. He walked into a club and there was a huge transvestite who tried to chat him up. His face went white and he was absolutely terrified! Coming from Sydney, I'm used to seeing drag queens because there's a huge gay population and all the best clubs and restaurants are mostly gay. You always go in groups and never go to the toilet on your own or get left on your own! English people are much more conservative.

Fabio was the telephone king. I'd love to see his phone bill, it must be huge. One night we were in a sports bar when his battery ran out, he'd been on so long. He then tried to borrow everyone else's. Only Viv was mug enough to let him and Fabio was off out the door. He was on the phone for hours.

It was a great trip for team morale. I wouldn't want to do it too often because it would harm your fitness but it's no bad thing every once in a while. I don't know any footballers that don't drink - except Merse (who didn't go on the

One of my earliest team photos. I dropped the silly grimace in later years.

With the Marconi youth team. Italian World Cup star Christian Vieri is fifth from left on the top row.

Meeting one of my heroes Pele with the Australian national youth team.

The local paper, the Evening Gazette, took this great picture on a visit to a Middlesbrough school.

Getting to grips with my little brother Daniel before a match at the Riverside.

Another Evening Gazette picture which they used at actual size to show the size of my hands.

Keeping another one out in training at Rockliffe Park.

Peter Shilton points me and Andy Dibble in the right direction.

A very dodgy wig that earned me the nickname Gloria at our Christmas party.

The rest of the lads in their Christmas disguises. How many can you spot?

A proud moment walking out behind John Pickering and Nigel Pearson at the Coca-Cola Cup Final.

We're there! Giving the lads a shower in the dressing room after securing promotion against Oxford.

Nigel gets the Boro equivalent of Gazza's famous dentist's chair celebration.

trip) and he's done enough of it. No-one got arrested so it was a good weekend. It was supposed to be a golfing trip as much as anything but not many people saw the golf course. The weather was foul, mind you!

Training the day after we got back was fun. It took us a good half-hour to get going. Some of the lads had to play in the reserves that night and they looked very ropey.

december 13th

Boro 4 Reading 0

Reading had us under pressure for the first 15 to 20 minutes and Nigel had to go off 20 minutes in. We held out well but it was tense game. It wasn't until 20 minutes to go that we broke through. Higgy scored a great goal and then the floodgates opened. Mikkel got two and Higgy got another. It was a little bit of a scare but once we were ahead we were all over them. It was just a question of how many.

It was a Seventies theme for the players' Christmas party. I managed to earn myself the new nickname "Gloria" after putting on a blonde wig. Everyone said I looked like Nicholas Lyndhurst when he dresses as a woman for the WH Smith's advert.

We got some funny looks walking through Middlesbrough town centre. There were quite a few dodgy moustaches, sideburns and curly wigs on view. Nigel was alright though - he just wore his usual gear. Merse looked great in his white suit. It was just a week after getting back from the Ireland trip so everyone was still in good spirits and had a good night. I couldn't face another big night out so soon so I left quite early.

The next day, Derek Whyte came in with a massive cut on the side of his head and his nose. I thought he must have been in a fight or something but he said he'd got home and all he could remember was going to the toilet. The next thing, he woke up with his wife standing over him and blood everywhere. Apparently, he'd passed out and hit his head on a radiator as he fell over!

The club organised for all the players to go out to some of the local hospitals to see the kids who are in before Christmas. Many of them would be there for the festive period itself and it's always sad to see sick kids.

Back in Australia we used to go to a special hospital for the terminally ill and that was really sad. Most of the kids in Middlesbrough weren't so bad but there was one who had just had a tumour removed from his brain and now had one in his spinal cord. It's great to see the smiles on the kids' faces when you see them but it just makes you glad that your own family are OK.

december 20th

Manchester City 2 Boro 0

I've never won at Maine Road and after going two goals down early on that was never going to change. City have shown before that they can get it together against the good teams and they should be a lot higher up the league than they are.

They just wanted it more than we did right from the start and it was all over in 20 minutes. The first goal was a penalty when Stampy went for the ball but collected the player first. There was no doubt about it. Then Paul Dickov got the second. It's disappointing because we could have gone three points clear at the top. It's a bit of a hiccup and we need to get back to winning ways right away.

I was actually on trial for a week and a half at Manchester City during Steve Coppell's brief time in charge. He said he wanted to sign me, my agent negotiated a fee with him and two days later Coppell resigned apparently because of illness. Apparently, their chairman said no and talked about taking me on loan.

There was a very strange atmosphere at the club. Coppell never appeared to me to be as unwell as he made out but he didn't seem right. Maybe it was just a way to get out. I spoke to him personally and one to one he seemed like he is now. But there were a lot of strange things going on behind the scenes at Man City.

They sent me a contract out to Germany with a figure missing off one of the fees we'd agreed. They rang me asking when I was going to sign. My fiance Paloma took the call. She told them that I wasn't signing for those terms. They then went over the contract again and rang back to tell me it was a typing error! I got a bad feeling about it and when Bradford came in, it was a complete contrast. City offered me more money but Bradford were more up front and things seemed much more settled. They also allowed me the get-out clause and it seemed right.

Derek Whyte is leaving the club to sign for Aberdeen. I'm disappointed to see him go because he's great for team spirit. He's a great, party guy and very popular with everyone at the club. I think he's a good footballer as well. But he wasn't getting a regular run in the side and has been out of contract since the summer.

Chris Freestone has also gone to link up with a fellow Australian of mine, David Seal, at Northampton. I used to play with him back in Australia. His father and my father used to stand on opposite sides of the pitch when we were nine or 10 years old and shout abuse at each other when we were playing. David's father coached the Penrith RSL team and my father coached my team and came to watch me play for Marconi where Seal also played.

Chris was always very quiet and looks a lot younger than he is. He needs first team football and should get it there. It seems a bit strange to let a striker go when we do lack cover but the gaffer obviously felt he was never going to be good enough. We have been linked with a lot of strikers but nothing seems to be going through. A lot of names haven't really excited me but Dion Dublin is one that I think would be a great signing.

Christmas was a bit better than usual because we weren't needed to train on Christmas Day. Playing on Boxing Day does tend to disrupt your life over Christmas but it was nice to have a little bit of time off. I trained on the morning last year with Bradford but I hadn't had to do it before. Over in Germany they have a two or three week break from football over Christmas and New Year. They play a lot less games over there and you notice the difference when you come to England.

december 26th

Huddersfield 0 Boro 1

It was very difficult conditions at Huddersfield. The pitch was mostly sand. We took time to get going but we pressured and pressured and eventually got the winner, an own goal from a corner. Huddersfield were a much improved team from when we played them earlier in the season and made it hard for us but we deserved to win in the end.

december 28th

Boro 3 Stockport 1

As usual over Christmas the matches have been packed in and we've had just one day off between games. After losing at home against them last season, we got a great victory over Stockport. We took the lead and I fancied us to go on and win it comfortably but then they equalised from a corner when a player wasn't picked up. Stockport aren't an easy side to play against but we came back in the second half and won the game with two goals from Mikkel.

After the game though none of the talk was about the result. Emerson hasn't returned from Brazil after being allowed home to spend Christmas with his family. We knew he wasn't going to play against Stockport, even though he had served his two match suspension, but he was supposed to be back to watch the game.

Everyone is surprised that he hasn't turned up. He seemed very happy when he went away and was talking about signing a new contract and staying at the club. He told everyone that, despite the speculation, he didn't want to play for Tenerife and was playing really well for us. Apparently, people are saying that the reason he hasn't come back is because he is waiting for the move there to be arranged. It's an exciting stage of the season and it seems a strange time for him to move. Tenerife are struggling at the bottom of the Spanish league and I wouldn't see it as a good move.

All the players are very disappointed with him. He's lost a lot of respect from us. He's done it before but we listened to his reasons. I feel sorry for the gaffer because he has laid his trust in Emerson and he has let Bryan, and us, down again. It seems that Emmo's agent basically tells him what to do. Emmo is an important member of the team and a great player. We will miss him if he doesn't come back but I think we all agree now that it is best if he does go.

chapter seven

New Year

With no game on New Year's Day, we were allowed out on New Year's Eve. It's a rarity in England to have the day off and most of the players took advantage of it. It's only three days to the next game so we couldn't go mad but it was nice to relax and have a few drinks.

It's not quite the same not going back to Australia to see my family but you never know I might ask the gaffer if I can go back next year. I quite fancy Christmas on Bondi Beach. That would be a good excuse for being late back!

January 3rd

QPR 2 Boro 2
FA Cup third round

We're back on the FA Cup trail after our trip to the final last season. Last year was incredible in the cups and I don't think people realise what an achievement it was to reach both finals. As I've said before it ended up being a disastrous season but it was so close to being a fantastic one.

While I was able to play in the Coca-Cola, I was cup-tied for the FA Cup. Ben Roberts came back in for the later rounds of the cup while I was playing the league games. Of course, I would have loved to play in an FA Cup Final but it didn't bother me that much to miss out on the cup games. I had a great cup run at Bradford and really enjoyed it. We beat Everton in the fourth round and then played Sheffield Wednesday, live on Sky, in the fifth. Those games probably gave me the media attention and gave me a bigger opportunity for people to see me. I'm sure they helped me to get the move.

I never really played a part in the build-up for the final and wasn't with the team much so I didn't get a real feeling of it. But the atmosphere on the day, and seeing the way Chelsea reacted afterwards, I could see how big a game it was.

Most players dream of reaching an FA Cup Final but last year's experience was far from fantastic for us. It was a funny sort of atmosphere, a very strange week. We had just been relegated and everyone was very low. The attitude was "let's just get this game over with".

Rav hadn't played in the last few league games and the big speculation in the media was about whether he was going to be fit or not. There was some resentment about his behaviour then but it all came out in the open when Neil Cox slagged Rav, the club and the supporters in the press.

Some of what Coxy said was right but the timing and manner of it was wrong. He should have had the intelligence to save it until after the game. Neil wasn't the only one feeling that way and he was angry about being out of the team.

Rav wanted to punch the hell out of Coxy at the hotel on the morning of the game and he was trying to do it again on the bus on the way to Wembley. It was appallingly bad timing and Coxy let himself and his team-mates down badly. He also let the club and the fans down. The fans had given him a hard time so he probably didn't feel any loyalty towards them. Also, he knew he was going to leave the club and had been dropped for the final but it was a selfish thing to do.

It didn't feel like an FA Cup Final. Coxy speaking in the papers and Rav reacting the way he did, I thought we were going to need a miracle to win the game. I knew before the game that we were going to have a very tough time and I think quite a few of the others felt the same. On the day, Chelsea were really focused and wanted the game more. When the goal went in in the first minute, it just typified the way things had been going.

Things didn't start too well at the start of what is hopefully another good cup run. We had another nightmare with the 'plane journey. The take-off was pushed back and we were thinking about going by train instead. In the end, when we did get to Heathrow the bus was late. We still got there on time but we didn't have much time to rest before the game and prepare.

We started the game a bit slowly and put ourselves under pressure with mistakes at the back. They took the lead from a quick throw. We picked up and started playing good football. We scored a cracker of a goal to equalise - it was like a training pitch goal, with a couple of great one-two's.

In the second half, they came at us again but we looked dangerous on the break. Jaime made a good run down the side and Robbie had an open goal. He was bragging about his great finish afterwards but I think he couldn't have missed. Unfortunately, they equalised late on and it's a replay back at the Riverside.

Emerson has finally come back after his extended stay in Brazil. He came into the training ground but got sent straight home again by the gaffer. He tried to act as if nothing had happened but no-one wanted to talk to him.

It's annoying because everything had been going so well. Last season was a disaster for off-the-field disturbances. For a couple of months now all that people have been talking about is what has been happening on the pitch. We've been making headlines with our football. We just hope things get sorted quickly so we can put this behind us.

January 6th

Reading 0 Boro 1
Coca-Cola Cup quarter-final

Curtis is having a rough trot. He must be cursing his luck. He's been to hospital twice in the last couple of weeks. The first visit came after an incident at the training ground. (No fighting with Rav this time!) Someone hit the ball at goal and Curtis managed to get in the way. He turned his head away and got hit on the ear. He had to go to hospital to have the blood removed with a syringe. He went out on New Year's Eve with a bandage around his head.

Next thing we know, Curtis wasn't able to travel to the game at Reading. He had been taken ill and rushed to hospital to have his appendix removed. Apparently, it wasn't the easiest of operations and he'll be out for at least six weeks.

Reading were really up for the game but we put in a good all-round performance and we're into the semi-finals of the Coca-Cola Cup again. There's still two games to go but there's no reason why we can't go back to Wembley.

It was touch and go whether the game would go ahead and it was a heavy pitch but we played pretty well. We should have won more comfortably but if you're going to score it might as well be in the last minute, there's no way back from that.

It was a controversial goal. It was difficult to understand what was going on as no-one could work out which way the referee was giving a free kick. Neil Maddison fouled their player but then the ref booked Trevor Morley, who must have said something. A scuffle broke out and the next thing we knew, the ref gave the free-kick our way and Maddo ran up to the ball and hit it long to Merse. Reading still had three defenders against two but Merse laid it off to Higgy and he finished it off.

Higgy was the man in demand after the game and was giving so many press interviews he got left behind! Alex Smith, the kit man, had told everybody about five times that we were going to leave as soon as possible so everyone got changed quickly and on to the coach. Vlad Kinder and Festa were on the coach and they don't even understand much English.

A guy from Sky asked me for an interview but I said we had to go. No-one expected anyone to disappear. Not all the players were going on the bus anyway so no-one thought anything of it when Higgy wasn't there.

Higgy loves the media and he got the chance to get to know them better - he spent five hours in a car driving up with a couple of the radio reporters. About 15 minutes into the journey, Higgy phoned up. We were just up the road but it was too late to turn round. We would have missed our flight. Higgy wasn't happy at all.

To make matters worse, he had left a bag on the plane which had his car park ticket in it for Teesside Airport. When he got there, in the early hours, he couldn't get his car out and had to follow really closely behind the reporter's car to sneak out. Apparently, they got caught by the security guards and had some explaining to do.

January 10th

Charlton 3 Boro 0

It was back down to earth with a bump at Charlton. We actually started the game well. They were nothing special but they pressurised us around the park and didn't stop running. On the day, they got what they deserved.

Their 'keeper never really had a save to make. Their first goal was a good one but I looked pretty stupid on the replay for the second. It looked like I'd flapped at it but their guy actually punched the ball out of my hands. We conceded a third when Merse lost control after we'd cleared a corner. It's a disappointing result but Charlton have a good home record and we need to make sure it's just one slip-up.

My brother Daniel has been training with the club's juniors. He played for the under-15 side this week and did quite well. He's already been to West Ham and Blackpool for trials and also to Millwall. I was just trying to get him out of the house!

He's definitely got the ability to make it but he seems to have a problem with his attitude. He thinks he's very cool. Whether he makes it or not will depend on whether he sorts out his attitude. The clubs he's been to have turned him down for that reason. Blackpool would definitely have taken him on otherwise.

Daniel might have a problem getting a work permit if he could get signed up here. He doesn't have a German passport like me but maybe I could sponsor him and be responsible for him. But he's only 15 and it would probably be better for him to stay in Australia for now.

The experience of rejection will probably be good for him in the long run. There's no reason why he can't come back in a year or two and try again.

Daniel's actually a lot better than I was at his age. He's learned from watching me train all the time when he was little and I used to kick around with him. He has a chance of making it.

Chris Kamara has been sacked by Bradford. I was very surprised but, listening to the chairman explaining his decision, they'd got 21 points from the last 20 games and he felt Chris wasn't going to turn it round. He never spent a lot of money which made it hard for Chris. A couple of the players he bought maybe didn't do as well as he would have hoped.

I always got on well with the chairman. Mind you, he got me for £150,000 and sold me a few months later for £1.25 million, with a pre-season friendly thrown in, so he was bound to get on with me. He did exceptionally well out of me.

I thought Chris had done a good job. He'd got them out of the Second Division, kept them in the First Division last season, going through a lot of players, and they had started really well this time. No-one expected them to be up among the leaders but maybe they started too well. They are actually now where most people would expect them to be but because they've slipped so badly the chairman thought it was for the best.

I spoke to Rob Steiner, a striker at the club, last month. He told me that Chris was under a lot of pressure and took it out on a few of the players. I've been on the receiving end of abuse from managers before and it's no fun. It must have been a tense atmosphere at the club.

I've no doubt that Chris will get another job. I still think he's got a good future ahead of him.

January 13th

Boro 2 QPR 0
FA Cup third round replay

QPR were crap. It was just a formality for us. A few young lads came in and played well but QPR were very poor. We had a tough game down there but this was easy and we're through to the next round.

Another young lad, Robbie Stockdale, came in for his debut at right-back. It was an outstanding debut, I don't think I've seen a better one from a young player. I knew nothing at all about him before the game but I was pleasantly surprised.

Emerson has completed his move to Tenerife after flying out to the Canary Islands. He came back into the training ground to say good-bye to everyone. It was a bit strange talking to him, a funny feeling. Again, he acted as if nothing had happened. Not many players spoke to him. I said a few words but not too much.

It does seem like a strange move to go to Tenerife. I think he's using it as a stepping stone. At the end of the day, if Tenerife go down and he moves to a big club in Spain, he'll get exactly what he wants. Only time will tell if it was the right move or not.

He made a few comments in the Press after leaving that didn't go down too well. It's always easy to say things after you've left because you know you're not going to bump into those people again. He certainly didn't say it while he was here. It shows a lack of character. He does seem to have been easily misled. A lot of people have said he was too easily influenced by his agent. He either had his own mind and opinion or he was too easily controlled.

Most of the time you create your own bad press. The press can treat players badly but if someone takes off two or three times then of course the press are going to give them a hard time. He brought most of the problems on himself. Emmo will be missed on the field and off it he was nowhere near as bad as Ravanelli, but he had pushed things too far and there was no way back.

January 17th

Boro 1 Ipswich 1

A very disappointing result. Festa was shown the red card but it wasn't a sending off for me. David Johnson went down when he was running through but I don't think Luca clipped him. It was a bit harsh. Even after that we managed to get one goal but we never managed to kill them off and they sneaked one back late on just as they had done in the away game.

January 24th

Boro 1 Arsenal 2
FA Cup fourth round

All the hype before the game inevitably was about Merse, playing against his old club. He's told the press that he actually considered giving up football completely earlier in the season when the travelling was getting to him. We all realised he had a problem but maybe we didn't appreciate how serious it was and how low he was feeling. He could whinge for England so we maybe didn't take him that seriously!

I don't think Merse realised how big a move it was coming to Middlesbrough. I was the same when I moved from Australia to Dresden in Germany and it can be hard to cope with such a massive upheaval in your life. Fortunately, he has had people around him who have helped him. Nigel Pearson definitely played a big part in persuading him to keep going. He's also got his brother Keith and friend Justin staying with him now and he's hoping to bring his family up in the summer. It's all worked out for the best with his recall to the England team and if we can win promotion it will prove to be a great move for him.

The game against Arsenal was quite disappointing. It wasn't a priority for us to go through in the cup but we still didn't give the game away. I thought the crowd were a bit harsh, they wanted a bit more from us. Anyone can turn round and say we let them play but they're a quality team and played really well especially in the first 20 minutes.

Everyone had that little bit of thought about what happened last season, a bit scared about the number of games we played. In the end we had a great chance to draw the game but a replay was the last thing we wanted. Maybe they wanted it a bit more than we did.

Andy Dibble's been brought in to the club until the end of the season. Ben's had a few problems with his back and been out for a long time so we needed another goalkeeper. Andy's a good trainer and has a lot of experience. Hopefully, from my point of view, he won't be needed but we do need cover should anything happen to me.

The gaffer has announced his retirement as a player. I thought he already had retired, to be honest, and he was only ever there for an extreme emergency. On the training pitch, he's still very physical and gets really involved but there comes a time when you have to decide if you want to continue training 100 per cent like everyone else does or you call it a day. To play and manage is too difficult, especially these days.

On the training pitch, it's John Pickering as first team coach who sets up all the exercises and games. He gets everything organised. Viv and the gaffer must talk about it beforehand but John leads things when we're training.

Everyone gets on really well with John. He gets a bit too serious sometimes and doesn't like getting stick from the boys. So we generally give him plenty to wind him up. He's the only one of the coaching staff who was here before the gaffer came in and you can see why he's been retained because he's very good.

I think Viv's main role is as a morale booster. He's very vocal and is really good for team spirit. He gets everyone going. He's always having side-bets with people at games. Everyone takes the Mickey out of him when he plays in training and he's always taking the Mickey out of everyone else. He makes things so much more enjoyable. It's not an easy thing to do. He also watches a lot of videos of our games and goes through things that went wrong and has a say on tactics.

January 27th

Liverpool 2 Boro 1
Coca-Cola Cup semi-final, first leg

We made an exceptional start to the game. Liverpool looked like they were lacking confidence. They were indecisive and played very poorly.

We scored first with a great goal by Merse and had we been able to hold on at 1-0 until half-time, who knows what could have happened. But Jamie Redknapp equalised with a great goal and they nicked it with another one near the end from Robbie Fowler.

It was disappointing to let it slip but we would have taken 2-1 at the beginning of the game so it was a great result to take back for the second leg. There's only one goal in it and all to play for.

Young Steve Baker did a man-marking job on Steve McManaman and played exceptionally well. There were reports afterwards saying that Bakes marked McManaman too aggressively but that was total nonsense because Bakes did a great job. There was some shirt-tugging and pawing but that happens in every game and McManaman gave as good as he got.

chapter eight

February

february 1st

Stoke 1 Boro 2

It was funny seeing Chris Kamara as he has just taken over at Stoke. I have some fond memories of working with him at Bradford and I'm not surprised that he got a job so quickly. He's got a tough job on his hands because they're a club that seem to be on the slide. They beat us early in the season but they've struggled to stay out of the relegation zone.

It was one of those games where we didn't play well. We took the lead and I thought we were all over them. They were under pressure and looked dead and buried but then there was a dodgy penalty decision given against Steve Baker. They could thank the referee really for getting them back in the game. But Jaime Moreno came on and got the goal that won it for us. It was a great finish.

Juninho has broken his leg. All the boys heard about it and felt sorry for him. He's a great guy and highly regarded. You don't wish that sort of thing on anyone, especially when it looks like he'll miss the World Cup. It was a horrendous tackle and looks like a serious injury. He'll be devastated if he misses the World Cup because he loves playing for Brazil and it's everyone's dream to play in a World Cup.

It's been made such a big thing that he had to leave England to play for Brazil. I think the manager has something against British football because he will pick players from the J League in Japan but not from England. I can't believe he thinks the J League is better than the Premier League.

February 4th

Boro 3 Tranmere 0

Tranmere came into the game with eight goalless draws in a row so we knew it would be difficult to break them down. Like a lot of sides, they came to the Riverside to put men behind the ball.

Michael Thomas came in for his debut after joining on loan from Liverpool. He did a good job, bringing a lot of experience into the team. He can hold the ball up very well, with a bit of arrogance in his play.

It took time to break them down but we got the result with three goals in the second half. Higgy broke the dead-lock and got another late on. Mikkel got the other.

February 7th

Birmingham 1 Boro 1

Birmingham built the game up as if it was a cup game and they were difficult opponents. We went 1-0 down early in match, due to our own mistake, and could have been two or three down in the first 20 minutes.

To our credit, we got our composure back and played a lot better. Luca scored a great goal, playing a one-two with Merse. Luca often seems to head off down the field and causes a bit of panic among his team-mates but he's fit enough to get back. In the second half, it was all down to us holding on but we defended well.

Jaime has gone back to Washington after his loan spell. The one thing he did do was score the winner against Stoke which could be crucial. Other than that though, he didn't show a great deal. He never really looked like he was going to do anything. He never broke into the team that much and I wasn't surprised to see him go. He's a nice guy who got on well with the lads but I think he came for the off-season just to play a few games, take it easy and see how it went.

The manager has spoken out in the press criticising people who've been spreading malicious rumours about some of the players. The lads were all very concerned about the rumours and the players involved were devastated. They couldn't understand where they had come from. It damages their reputations even when it's not true. There are a lot of naive people out there who actually believe these things and carry them on.

For people to start up stories that are so malicious and childish is unbelievable. It's something that happens, I suppose. I've come across rumours before but none as nasty as these. I had a young kid repeat one of the stories to me. I couldn't believe one of our supporters was doing it.

Hopefully with Bryan criticising the people spreading the gossip, everything will quieten down. I think it was the right thing to do and it should put an end to it. We're doing well and pushing for promotion, so the last thing we need is something that's going to ruin morale or confidence.

We've signed a Colombian striker called Hamilton Ricard. Nobody knows anything about him. We've read and heard reports but that's all. There seems to be some doubt about whether he'll get a work permit or not but we'll have to see what happens.

The manager doesn't come in and tell us when we've signed a new player, we usually read it in the papers or hear it from one of the other players or coaching staff.

We've always known we needed more strike power. Hopefully this will really strengthen the squad. We've been incredibly lucky that Merse and Mikkel haven't got injured. They've got 30 goals between them and you can't argue with that record.

February 14th

Boro 1 Bradford 0

It was good to play against my old team. I've always got on well with the supporters and they gave me another good reception. You're never quite sure how they're going to react but they were excellent with me.

It was a poor game and we didn't play well after playing so many games in the last week. But Higgy snatched the goal and we came away with the points. Higgy's got quite a few this season and has a great ability to get into the right positions. He's a good finisher and has an excellent record for a midfielder.

The win puts us back on top of the table and it sets us up nicely for the next games, against Liverpool and Sunderland, though we know we have to play better to beat them.

The standard of the pitch at the Riverside isn't making it easy for us to play good football. It has been a nightmare to play on in the last few weeks. One week it's wet and soggy with loads of sand on it and the next it's rock hard.

Kicking is almost impossible. I got a back pass in the game that I mis-hit. Luckily, I recovered but it's difficult when the ball's bobbling all over the place when it's running back to you. Sometimes you don't get the chance to control the ball if a forward's running at you. I might only get one kick every 10 minutes and that makes it difficult.

Before the game, we heard that we'd completed the signing of Alun Armstrong from Stockport. I don't really know him as a player. He has scored something like 15 goals for Stockport but the only player I remember from there is Brett Angell because he's such a big guy and strong in the air. But Armstrong's record shows that he can score goals and he should be a good inclusion to the squad. He was brought out on to the pitch and introduced to the crowd at half-time in the game which was a bit unusual.

February 18th

Boro 2 Liverpool 0
Coca-Cola Cup semi-final, second leg

Another new striker has arrived - the third in a week! The Italian Marco Branca is the latest. We're not surprised because it has been quite an issue for a couple of weeks with speculation about whether or not he would come to the club.

He's a good friend of Gianluca's and Luca wasn't even sure whether he would come or not. It's good to have it sorted out. After a lot of stories about players turning us down, it's nice to have some positive news for a change.

Branca started training with us on the day before the Liverpool cup game, and we knew straight away that he would be playing. We had a practice game and he was in the team so it was clear that he would be starting.

The gaffer told the press that he wouldn't be playing. We thought it was a bit strange but I think it was designed to take the pressure off Marco. It also meant that Liverpool weren't expecting him. Having Paul Ince, a former team-mate of his in the side, Liverpool would have known a bit about him but it must have taken them by surprise when the team-sheets were handed in three-quarters of an hour before the game.

The atmosphere of the crowd as we ran out was amazing. In the dressing room you don't really know what it's like out on the pitch. People told me later about the classical music, the flag-waving and the build-up and it was electric when we ran out.

Once the game had kicked off, I didn't know whether to jump up and down or not. We'd only played four minutes, I hadn't touched the ball and we were 2-0 up. All I could think was that we had to hang on for 86 minutes. But defensively and all around the pitch it was a tremendous performance, they never really looked like they could get back into it. Branca had an incredible debut, scoring after just four minutes. His all-round game was excellent and he looks a good buy already.

The atmosphere this time was a bit different from last year when we beat Stockport to get to the final. We had a bit of a scare in that game when they scored but the feeling at the end was more relief than anything else because everyone expected us to win. We were the favourites after beating them 2-0 in the away leg.

This time it was a bigger sensation having beaten Liverpool. It wasn't that we didn't expect to beat them, just that everyone had written us off. We knew we could get through but it was down to how we performed on the night.

The one thing we are thinking now is that we want to win the cup this time. It's a tremendous achievement to make it to three cup finals in a row but we don't want to be remembered as the team that lost three consecutive cup finals. It's the perfect opportunity to play Chelsea and make up for last year.

It was a tremendous occasion and the crowd was unbelievable. We came back out and did a lap of the pitch. It was an amazing feeling. There was a bit of champagne sprayed around in the dressing room but no-one was getting carried away with a big league game ahead against Sunderland. That game's even more important.

Last season after we played big cup games we often played dreadfully in the next match. This season that hasn't happened so much. I think we've got more consistency in the team now and being at the top of the table has given us confidence. Only being in one cup has helped as well.

Beating Liverpool will give us even more confidence and if you're not up for a promotion battle against your main north-east rivals then there's something wrong.

February 21st

Boro 3 Sunderland 1

The atmosphere when we played up at the Stadium of Light was tremendous and this time it was fantastic again, a continuation of Wednesday night. I think the crowd was still partying.

We took time to find our feet in the game but I never really felt threatened. Branca scored two great goals and to score three in his first two games is excellent. Alun Armstrong came off the bench and scored a great goal on his debut as well.

I never thought Sunderland were going to score all game and I was a bit disappointed to lose the clean sheet in the last minute. There was a lapse of concentration and we fell asleep at the back. Keeping clean sheets means a hell of a lot to me. Before the game I usually look in the programme to see how many goals I've conceded. I strive to concede as few as possible.

There was a piece in the programme recently saying my goals per game record is one of the best in the club's history. My record so far is pretty good, less than a goal a game, but I've only made a few appearances and when I've played more I can really compare. It's nice to know that I've got off to a good start though.

February 25th

Boro 1 Crewe 0

There was definitely a feeling in the crowd before the game that we'd beaten Liverpool and Sunderland so beating Crewe was just a formality. The fans have been demanding this season, thinking that we should rip through the lesser teams. It isn't often that easy. Most teams have come to the Riverside and put men behind the ball trying to frustrate us.

Crewe actually put in one of the best away performances I've seen by any team at the Riverside this season. Their away record is good and they could easily have got something from the game. They're a good young football playing team, one of the only ones in the division.

Neil Maddison got our goal with a great header from a corner but they had a goal disallowed late on for offside. I couldn't say whether it was or not because by that point I was in a lot of pain.

Earlier on, the ball had come through towards me. As I went out to punch it clear, I connected with the ball and a player's head at the same time. The ball looped up in the air and, as I got up from the ground, I tried to turn back towards the goal. Straight away I felt my groin go.

For about two weeks I've had problems with my groin. The tendon that runs down from my pelvis to the top of the thigh muscle was enflamed and aggravated but it wasn't going to stop me playing. In the end something had to give and I suffered a partial tear of my groin. I knew straight away there was more to it than before. When I injured it previously there was nowhere near as much pain. I was struggling to run and kick the ball. There was only about 15 minutes to go and with no 'keeper on the bench, I had to stay on. Afterwards, I went straight into the dressing room and got ice on the injury.

A scan has shown a tear and I've been told it could take from three to six weeks, depending how bad the tear is. I'm hoping, because it's only a partial tear, that it will be only three. I'm aiming to be back in time for the Norwich game which is a week before the Coca-Cola Cup final. I don't like missing any games but that's one I desperately don't want to miss.

chapter nine

March

I'm in every day for treatment. Even when the players are off I'm in seven days a week. It's annoying and boring as hell. Being injured always is.

The treatment I'm getting is laser, ultra-sound, electrode and what we call a fresh air machine which puts out magnetic waves. I'm sat strapped to all these machines for half an hour each and it's incredibly tedious.

In my place, Andy Dibble will come into the side. As a 'keeper you know that if you get injured somebody else will come in and you could find it hard to get your place back. Andy will have his chance in the next few games.

I never want to miss a game. I was unfortunate enough to miss the first six games of the season and I thought I'd had my share of injuries. Things were going really well and I was looking forward to playing for the rest of the season.

Of course, I want the team to do well even without me. But I believe in the gaffer and that he regards me as number one. If someone comes in and does well in my absence then all well and good but I'm still confident that I can get back into the side.

Ben Roberts is very disappointed that he can't take advantage of my injury to get another chance. He's had big problems all season with a back injury and he's pulled up lame again. He came back into training this week but after four days he's out again. I'd be surprised if he's fit again this season. He last trained in December and it's very frustrating for him.

I tuned in to Sky to watch our game against Nottingham Forest but wasn't prepared to see us get a real hiding, 4-0. It was unfortunate for Andy coming in for his debut but, in all fairness, you can't put the blame just on him. He said to me afterwards that he felt he could have done better for their first goal but it was a poor performance by the whole team.

It's hard to explain how you can beat Liverpool and Sunderland and then get beaten by such a margin. There wasn't a single Boro player who came out of the game with any credit.

After the Forest defeat it's an even bigger surprise to get thrashed 5-0 by QPR. I listened to the game on the radio and I couldn't believe what I was hearing.

QPR are a quality side on paper but they'd won just one in 16. They got a lucky goal when Steve Vickers screwed the ball into his own net but from then on the floodgates opened, which is really uncharacteristic for us this season. In previous games we've gone a goal down but have always come back to get something from the game.

Andy must be devastated. He was thrilled to get the chance to play but then we go and get beat 4-0 and 5-0. I've never been part of a team that's had that happen before. Hopefully we can get it sorted quickly.

The players have been given a few days off after the game. Some people might criticise that and say they should be in the next day but I think the players need to get away, clear their heads and get refreshed for the next game. We've got the weekend off because Wolves, who we were due to play, are involved in a cup quarter-final so it gives us time to get things right.

I've received a fax from the Australian Soccer Federation. It says that Australia is regarded as one of the best footballing nations in the world at the moment (!) and that if players are selected they must play.

I couldn't believe they'd sent me one after everything that's happened. I wasn't included in any of the recent squads and there has been a bit of an outcry about what I said so I thought I wouldn't be a part of things anymore, especially while Terry Venables is still involved.

The Venables situation has become an absolute joke. It's clear to everyone that he is going to leave. It just shows the naivety of the Federation. They're being made to look ridiculous by the way Venables is touting himself around looking for jobs and they keep insisting that they want to keep him.

Merse has stated publicly that he'd like to stay at the club for the rest of his five year contract and eventually become manager. He's got a lot more playing days ahead of him yet but it's one of his ambitions.

There are certain players that you think would be really good as managers. Whether they want to do it or not is another thing. Nigel Pearson is one that stands out and I think he would very good. Whether he becomes successful or not isn't just down to his ability. There's a lot of other things involved in success, like the club you go to, the finances available, the players at the club and so on. Andy Townsend could also go into management and maybe Robbie Mustoe.

I certainly won't be doing it. When I finish playing football that will be it. I might end up coaching my local under-10's or 12's but that will be it. I can't understand why some players are desperate to go into management. There's so many people who were remembered as great players but are now known for failing as managers. They say supporters are fickle but it's not just them, it's everyone connected with football and the media. I'd rather just stop playing and become a beach bum!

After the last two defeats, the gaffer has gone out and bought another 'keeper - Marlon Beresford. The first thing I knew about him signing was when he was here. I'd never heard of him beforehand. They say he's one of the better 'keepers in the Second Division. All I can say is that he'd want to be. Marlon came in for his debut against Swindon and he did quite well. To be fair he didn't really have anything to do in a 6-0 win.

I spoke to Andy Dibble and he's a bit disappointed about how things have gone. He's just trying to keep his head up and keep going. There's no point sulking and he's old enough and experienced enough to know that. He's a good pro.

We desperately needed the win against Swindon after what had happened before. I was never too worried because our home form has been excellent. We are a different team now. At the start of the season, it was the other way round, we were better away, but now I feel we're almost unbeatable at home.

Swindon are not the team they were last year. When we played them away, they were top of the table and it was their first defeat in a couple of months but since then they've struggled and hardly won a game. Even though they're a poor side, it was a big surprise to win 6-0. The bookmakers had us at something like 66-1 to do that and apparently quite a few fans bet on it and they couldn't pay out on the day.

Hamilton Ricard was introduced to the crowd at half-time after getting his work permit. I haven't seen him yet, not having trained. As well as the injury I've been off ill with a sinus infection and missed seeing the Swindon game. The lads say Ricard is strong and fast, a bit awkward like Paulo Wanchope at Derby, but effective.

I didn't go to our game at Portsmouth because I was in getting treatment again. I listened to the game on the radio and Marlon did well, saving a penalty to keep it 0-0. I've only faced a couple of penalties, one in my first league game against Sheffield Wednesday and then one against Stoke and I haven't saved one yet. Marlon is supposed to be the penalty king, saving more than he lets in.

We're being linked with a move for Paul Gascoigne. Like everyone else, us players only know what's in the papers. No-one's really talking about it because we've been linked with so many players but it would be an interesting one if he does come.

I've been back running and training for the last couple of days. I've been doing some handling with a medicine ball as well as getting all the treatment. My major problem would be kicking the ball.

The gaffer gave me the option whether to play or not against Norwich but I didn't feel 100 per cent and the last thing we need is for me to break down and miss the cup final. With Andy and Marlon cup-tied and Ben injured I'm the only available 'keeper. Peter Shilton has registered himself just in case.

We had a similar problem for last season's FA Cup Final. I was injured, so was Gary Walsh and Ben was carrying a knock so the gaffer looked at signing Peter Shilton then but he was cup-tied. In the end, Ben had to play.

It would have been a bit risky to play against Norwich. Marlon did OK again - another clean sheet - and we won 3-0. Hamilton came in for his debut and looked quite promising. He didn't score but caused a few problems.

Mikkel came on and got the third goal and looked really delighted. He's scored plenty of goals this season but has lost his place since the new strikers have come in. I always thought we needed another striker even though Becky and Merse had done well. If one of them had got injured we would have had big problems and we needed the competition. Buying three at the same time was a bit of a surprise but Branca and Armstrong have looked really impressive since joining.

But I feel for Mikkel. It's not just because I'm good friends with him because I feel for anyone else in that position. I felt for Ben Roberts when I came back from injury and took his place. But things like that happen and you just have to get on with it. I have been in that situation before myself and there aren't many players that haven't at some time.

chapter ten

The Cup Final

march 29th

Boro 0 Chelsea 2
Coca-Cola Cup final

I didn't have the best training week form-wise in the lead-up to the big game. In fact I had a nightmare. Everything that could go wrong did but I was still confident that when it came to the big day I would be ready. It was understandable having missed four or five weeks and I didn't really feel 100 per cent until the day of the game.

Leading up to the game, the gaffer kept telling me not to do anything silly and make sure I only did what I had to do. But if you try and be too careful you can get injured so I just got on with my normal routine. You just have to stop when you've done enough and not overdo it.

In the end, I was more worried about my ankle than the groin injury. I strained a tendon in the ankle on Friday, the day before the game, just from kicking. It was the first time I'd kicked a ball. Fortunately, I knew straight away it wasn't serious enough to stop me playing but I had an injection before the game and I was fine.

The build-up didn't really pick up until the Thursday when we had a press conference at the stadium. It was a bigger one this year than last mainly because of the signing of Paul Gascoigne. In the eyes of the media that was the main story and it took the attention away from the rest of the lads who the club had already arranged to be there to talk about the cup final.

We'd heard rumours about Gazza coming for a few weeks but after so many players being linked with us we weren't taking it too seriously. On Tuesday, we heard that he had decided to come but it wasn't until Wednesday when he turned up for training that we knew for real that he was coming.

He's a great signing and a great boost for the club. He showed straight away that he's different class on the training pitch. The first day was unbelievable with all the press turning up at the training ground. Fortunately, the stewards kept them out and we could get on with training.

He seems very quiet and friendly - nothing like the picture you get of him from the media. It was difficult for him to come in not really knowing anyone, especially ahead of such a big game, but he's settled in well.

After the press conference on Thursday we left for London the next day. Last year we left earlier but it was a bit too early and there was too much time in the hotel.

We trained on Friday morning and flew down on the afternoon. Nothing special happened at the hotel. Everybody has their own routines on away trips and different things they like to do. I go to my room to relax, watch TV and rest. On the Saturday, we trained in the morning, came back, had some lunch and rested in the afternoon, watching TV.

On a match day, I usually go down for breakfast or stay in the room and order room service for breakfast. I generally relax or go for a walk and then go down for the pre-match meal. Some lads get up early, others lie in bed until around 11.00. I couldn't do that because I wouldn't feel fresh enough for the game but everyone is different.

We set off for Wembley a bit earlier this year, at about 12.30. In a way it's like any other game but you're all dressed up in your suits and then you see the Twin Towers and you start to feel the nerves.

It's a huge buzz every time you go there. Just seeing the supporters as you drive up and then when you go out on to the pitch is amazing. It's a fantastic feeling. It's a bit of a strange atmosphere when you first get there because the stadium's only half full. We went out and had a look around, watched a bit of the celebrity game and then went back into the dressing room.

The gaffer gave his team talk, telling us there's no point having a great day out and spoiling it by losing the match. He said that nobody remembers the losers, only the winners, and that we owed them one after last year. He told us to go out and do our best, saying if we all did our best we could beat them.

In the first 20 minutes, half-hour, I thought we were probably the better team. I made a couple of saves. I can remember Mark Hughes having a shot. You know when you've made a good save and he looked surprised that I'd kept it out.

In the second half, we dropped off a bit. I felt we could snatch it with a couple of half-breaks but as it went on we looked less likely to score. When it came to extra-time, I thought our only chance would be penalties, I couldn't see us scoring. As soon as they scored, I knew it was over. I couldn't see us coming back.

A lot of people said they thought the ball had gone out before Dennis Wise crossed it for the goal but I never thought that. I was disappointed I didn't save the header because I got a good hand to it and almost kept it out but it was just a bit too hard. It was a downward header and skipped off the grass.

Maybe tiredness played its part after a tough schedule and long season but Chelsea have a lot of experienced players who are playing week in week out at the top level in the Premiership and Europe and that probably made the difference.

When the final whistle goes, you just want to get off the pitch and into the dressing room. It's not a great feeling to go up and get a losers' medal and then to watch them lift the trophy and the crowd going berserk.

The Middlesbrough fans were fantastic yet again. Before the game, during and even after, they out-sang Chelsea and gave us great support. It was a big shame for them to lose yet again.

Gazza gave his medal to Craig Hignett who was left out of the 14. It showed his true character. Whatever others might say, it proves he does care and is one of the boys. It was a nice touch. There was no bitterness about Gazza coming into the team. We all wanted to win the game and to do that you need the best team possible. No-one doubts that he's a great player and he could have won us the game. Of course, it's hard for Higgy but the manager has a job to do and some players have to miss out.

One of the great things about the cup final was that my Dad came over to see me play. It was the first time he'd seen me play in Europe. He'd seen me on TV back in Australia but it was great to have him there. He enjoyed it and, having watched me through all the junior ranks, it was a proud moment to see me play at Wembley in a cup final.

After the game, we went back to our hotel and then on to the Royal Lancaster Hotel for an after-match dinner. It wasn't as bad as last year after the FA Cup Final when everyone was very down. This time, we all felt it was a tremendous achievement to get to the final and that we had put up a better show against Chelsea this time round. Also, last year we were relegated while now at least we have a promotion challenge to look forward to.

I'm just kicking myself because we would have been in Europe if we had won. It would have been unbelievable to be back in the Premier League and playing in Europe. It's always been one of my biggest dreams.

I sat on the bench when I was at Kaiserslautern in European games and it's not the same as playing but it was still a great experience. We played Slovan

Bratislava, Vlad Kinder was playing for them, then Real Betis and, in the next year, Red Star Belgrade in the Cup Winners' Cup. I went to Belgrade and there were 70,000 fanatical people in a big old stadium. It was a tremendous atmosphere. It's something I want to experience again.

Chapter Eleven

April

The atmosphere is quite good back at Rockliffe. It's almost as if we haven't played at Wembley. We're straight back into things looking ahead to the promotion run-in.

Gazza's friend, Jimmy "Five Bellies" Gardiner, has been getting a bit of stick after being pictured leaving court with Merse. Merson had been fined for speeding and Jimmy had gone along with him to give him support. But one of the papers had printed a three page spread with the line "The picture that should set alarm bells ringing for Boro and England". Everyone thought it was quite funny and there were a few jokes about Jimmy being a bad influence.

Jimmy's at the training ground every day and he's no problem at all. If someone wants to have a mate there then why not? I've had people come up and watch us train, eat in the cafeteria or whatever and everyone else has. If Gazza and Merse want to have people there all the time then it's no problem as far as I'm concerned. It doesn't interfere with the training or the players.

It was so typical of the press to come out with a story like that. With two big personalities like Merson and Gazza we are going to get a lot of attention and it would make news whatever Merse was in court for with his past history. But there was nothing to make of it.

Following Gazza's arrival, Michael Thomas has gone back to Liverpool. There was talk of us signing him at one stage and he's a quality player but we have an abundance of midfielders. He showed that he's solid and can play the ball as well. He's quite similar to Robbie Mustoe. He's more of a players' player than a fans' player because he doesn't stand out but he works hard for the team. Those are usually the ones that get overlooked.

April 4th

West Brom 2 Boro 1

I honestly thought that everyone had got over Wembley but the game against West Brom was awful. We played poorly. Basically they were up for it and we weren't. They wanted it more than we did. Maybe we were still caught up in the cup final. One minute you're playing against Chelsea at Wembley, the next you're back in the First Division playing at West Brom.

West Brom took the lead from a penalty. It should never have been given. From the corner of my eye, all I saw was the guy falling over and Robbie standing next to him. Robbie said at half-time that the guy had taken a swipe at him and he had kicked him back. The referee was only 10 yards away from it all and really should have given a free kick to us and maybe booked Robbie for retaliating. But that left us on the back foot straight away and they scored again early in the second half.

We only played well in the last 20 minutes after we had pulled a goal back. We actually could have snatched a draw at the end when Hamilton had a good opportunity and sliced it into the crowd.

After the games, the gaffer hasn't usually had to have a go at us but after this one he had good reason to. He felt that we hadn't performed at all and that we'd let everyone down. We just know that we can't afford any more performances like this one.

Nobody goes out to have a bad game but maybe some people were too relaxed, thinking we've played Chelsea and were unlucky to lose so all we need to do is turn up to beat West Brom. Albion have had a disappointing second half to the season and wanted to make up for that.

We're all very disappointed and it puts us in more danger of going into the play-offs. That's the last thing we want to do after being in the top two for most of the season.

April 7th

Sheffield United 1 Boro 0

I thought it was one of our better away performances this year but it's another disappointing result. The attitude was there but the finishing wasn't. We really could have had six or seven goals.

Hammo missed some unbelievable chances. It's obviously frustrating for everyone else who's worked to create the chances but you can't just blame him. Merse missed a penalty as well and we had other chances. Everyone on the pitch takes their share of the blame.

Everyone gets on really well with Hamilton and we all know you can go through phases, especially as a striker, when nothing goes right for you. It can't be easy for him when he's just come to a new club and a new country and hopefully it will come good for him.

I was very disappointed with the goal. I can't understand how I dropped the ball and gave it to Dean Saunders who just tapped it in. I was a little bit worried about falling back into the net but it's one of those things you can't really explain. You just have to make sure it doesn't happen again. It hasn't really happened to me all season and it's disappointing that it meant we lost the game.

After this result, I can't help feeling that promotion might be slipping away from us. Sunderland are now five points ahead of us. All we can do is knuckle down and try and get as many points as we can and hope it's enough.

The play-offs would be a very difficult way to get into the Premier League. You have three other teams there which have had good runs towards the end of the season while we would have been losing or drawing to drop into the play-off zone. Playing home and away or in a one-off game at Wembley anything can happen. After a long, hard season we want to get promoted on the last day of the season and not have to worry about the play-offs.

All the press stories are saying that the arrival of Paul Gascoigne is to blame for our recent slump in form. It seems that ever since Gazza arrived that's all the media want to talk about but no-one takes it seriously. It's total rubbish.

One player can't come in and make such a big difference to a team. Overall the team has not been performing to the level it should be.

You only need to see Gazza on the training pitch to know what a phenomenal player he is. You can see how comfortable he is on the ball, he always wants it. His finishing, passing, running with the ball and everything is excellent. At the end of the day, he's a world class player and will be an asset to the club.

There have always been reports about what Gazza has done off the pitch. But as long as he performs on it, that doesn't matter. And I have found him totally different to how the media portrays him. I can only take him as I find him and so far he has been first class. He joins in with the humour in the dressing room and gets on really well with everyone.

April 11th

Boro 4 Bury 0

The gaffer said before the game that he was setting us a target of winning all our last six games. It's going to be tough but, looking at the run-in, it's something we can do.

We got off to the right start by comfortably beating Bury. By no means are they an easy team to play. They took the lead recently against Sunderland and only lost 2-1 in the end. They stack their defence and are very good on the counter-attack. But there was clearly a gap in class.

We played well to beat them 4-0. I didn't have much to do in the game. Hammo got his first goal which should be good for his confidence and Marco responded to being left out against Sheffield United by getting a hat-trick. His first one was a particularly outstanding goal. He's shown since he's been here that he's an excellent goal-scorer.

april 13th

Reading 0 Boro 1

With two games in three days, you just spend the day in between relaxing, getting a rub-down and massage, maybe a jog. There's not much you can do.

Reading are by no means an easy team to play away from home. Even so, I think they're one of the poorest teams we've played this season and they look doomed now.

For the first 25 minutes we were a class above them and got the goal through Marco. After that we let it slip again. Maybe it was tiredness creeping in but we didn't kill the game off. The 'keeper made some good saves and we missed some good chances and it put the pressure back on us. I had a couple of not particularly difficult saves to make at the end and I was pleased to get the clean sheet.

Higgy came back into the side for the Bury game and unfortunately got sent off late on against Reading. He's been bitterly disappointed not to be involved recently and he's been raring to go. But he probably wanted to do too much and got carried away. Fortunately, it was late on and didn't matter too much.

Higgy's had a contract dispute with the club going on for some time now. He's out of contract at the end of the season and has been made an offer and, whoever is to blame, he's turned that down. I'm not sure whether that's the reason for him being left out or not but when he gets the chance he wants to play. He's not the sort to just stop playing. It would be a shame to lose him because he's a talented player but I suppose the gaffer has to decide what he feels a player is worth.

We're level on points now with both Sunderland and Charlton. We still need Sunderland to drop points because they've scored more goals than we have but if we can win the last four we must have a good chance. Sunderland have still got some difficult away games, including one at Ipswich, whilst we've got three out of four at home.

Charlton are also in it but they have played a game more so if we can win all our games it doesn't matter what they do. They're a good side especially at home but I wouldn't say they're particularly excellent. They're a solid team who work hard together. They've got Mendonca up front who's scored plenty of goals and there's a great appetite among the players.

Gazza and Merse have both been called up by England for the friendly game against Portugal. It's good news for them and with Gazza back playing week in, week out again he must go to the World Cup. England need him. He's definitely got more to offer than any other English midfielder.

Merse has done consistently well all year and deserves his place too. He didn't play that well in the last England game against Switzerland but no-one really did and he got the equalising goal and played well in the last B-team game. I think both of them should go to France.

Mikkel looks like he will miss out though. It's a shame for him because he's played the majority of the season and was leading scorer for most of it. I am the closest to him in the club and I can see how much it hurts him. Twelve months ago he was playing in the Denmark team but he knows that he won't go to France if he's not playing here and he hasn't been getting the chances recently.

My own international horizons have not brightened too much. I've been looking out in the mailbox but, surprisingly, I haven't been invited to play in

Terry Venables farewell game. To be fair, I wouldn't want to play because I've had nothing but bad experiences with him and I'm glad he's going. It looks certain that he'll go to Crystal Palace now and hopefully it will mean a shake-up within the national set-up over in Australia.

April 17th

Boro 1 Manchester City 0

It was a very hard game but I expected that because they are fighting for survival and we desperately needed the points. There was also Jamie Pollock coming back to his old club and wanting to prove a point. He certainly talks a good game!

The biggest talking point was the sending off of Steve Vickers. The referee decided that he had head-butted Lee Bradbury so showed him the red card. Steve was a bit silly to go towards him with his head and he did nudge him a bit but the guy clearly took a dive.

There were a few challenges flying around in our league game at Maine Road and they were up for it more than us then. This time, we refused to let them bull-doze us and gave as good as we got. We had that extra bit of quality and went a goal up through Alun Armstrong after some great work by Gazza. The sending-off could have changed things but they never really created anything. I didn't have a save to make all game.

There was a lot of talk about what happened at half-time when a few people confronted each other in the tunnel. Our old friend Pollock was at the centre of it. The most disappointing thing was that I missed it all! By the time I got there it was all over. That's the disadvantage of being at the far end of the pitch ...

April 24th

Port Vale 0 Boro 1

It was really difficult conditions, the pitch was very heavy, one of the worst we've played on for a while. Port Vale are another side looking for points to steer clear of relegation. It was our last away game of the season and the win sets us up nicely for the two remaining home games.

We got off to a fantastic start with a goal inside the first two minutes from Merse. It turned out to be the winner in the end but it was a difficult match. It was probably my busiest game of the season but I haven't really had too many of those so you don't mind having a few games like that now and then.

Of course, you're happy to keep them out and keep a clean sheet. They had two good chances late on but you have to be alert the whole game. I was pleased with the saves I made. You spend all the time training for various situations and it's nice when they come off on the pitch. It was great to be named man of the match on Sky TV but more importantly it was a clean sheet and another three points.

After the second save, a one-on-one, Gazza shouted something from the bench and I responded with a gesture imitating someone smoking a cigar. It's one of those ongoing things that we've all been doing recently - it just means "easy" or "no problem". I was actually caught doing that on the Sky cameras and everyone was asking me about it after the game.

For the second week running, Sunderland played on Saturday after we played a Friday night game. I did look out for their result but really wasn't expecting Sunderland to drop any points against Crewe last week or Stoke this week and they won both games. The game all the players are waiting for is the one against Ipswich. That will be the tough match and could give us the chance to close the gap. But if they win that, it will be all over bar the shouting. I'll definitely be watching that on Sky.

On Sunday, Forest beat Reading. That's them definitely up now as far as I'm concerned. We would have to win both our games by huge scores and they would have had to lose against Reading and then against West Brom on the last day of the season. For me they were up three or four weeks ago and they would have had to drop off badly. We've just been concentrating on that one remaining promotion spot and the battle with Sunderland and Charlton.

I think as a whole the English First Division is a much higher standard than those in other countries. The German equivalent, the Second Division, is a lot weaker. This division is very difficult to get out of and even though there are four teams that are building up a massive number of points, the overall standard is pretty good.

Forest, Sunderland and Charlton all have an advantage over us because they have scored more goals. The Nationwide League works on that rather than goal difference when teams are level on points. Most players think that's ridiculous and I agree. The game's about defending as well as attacking. I just look back to the game we lost 5-0 to QPR. If we had lost that game 5-2 we would have actually gone top of the league. That's just ridiculous. I don't understand why the Nationwide League works on goals scored. It would be devastating to miss out because of a rule change. With two games to go, we just have to make sure it doesn't come down to that but it's going to go right to the wire.

chapter twelve

The Final Push

Luca Festa has won the Supporters Club player of the year award. He hasn't been making too much fuss about it. I couldn't make it to the awards night because my mother and my grandmother have been over here for a couple of weeks and they were leaving that night. My father was over for the cup final but could only stay for a week because that's all the time he could get off work. Then my mother and grandmother came over for 10 days while Mum was visiting Germany.

Luca has had a good season and deserves the award. My own player of the year would probably be Nigel but I'm sure Merse will also be in contention when the official player of the year is decided.

Festa has been in ecstasy since his buddy Marco came over. Branca seems a nice, genuine guy and nothing like Ravanelli. He tries to speak English and the boys appreciate that. Festa used to hang around with Rav quite a lot and maybe got tarred with the same brush a bit. But since he's gone we've got to know the real Festa. He is a funny guy and Branca and him are always trying to out-do each other with their English. Luca's also signed his life away with a new five year deal at the club.

I received a fax from the Australian Soccer Federation asking me to "notify the ASF of my availability as a possible squad member on the 6th June." The 6th of June already has an important entry in my diary because that's when I'm getting married. I don't think it would have gone down too well with my fiance if I'd asked her to put the wedding back.

In any case, I'm having the plate removed from my leg as soon as the season's over so I won't be fit enough to take part. Hopefully, we won't be in the play-offs so I'll be able to go into hospital next week.

Meanwhile, another player seems to have fallen out with the Australian Soccer Federation. Leeds' striker Harry Kewell was due to play for the national team on a Saturday but pulled out because he was injured. Leeds were playing on the Monday and by that time he was fit enough to play. That sort of thing happens all the time in football and a couple of days really can make all the difference.

But the Federation exercised their right to stop him playing for Leeds. They had wanted him to fly out for the game even though he was injured. I think they just wanted him there to boost their ticket sales. He's a high profile player and a big crowd draw so they were just thinking about their own pockets rather than what's best for the player. Understandably, the player and the club were unhappy about it and Kewell's now threatening not to play in their Olympic side.

The timing of the Australian matches is a joke. They know the dates of all the Premier League games and when the international breaks are but they arrange their games at completely different times so players have to miss league games. They insist that clubs have to release their players because it's FIFA regulations.

Looking back now, I'm glad I didn't get selected earlier in the season because I would have missed loads of games and then wouldn't have even sat on the bench. Kalac probably would have been ahead of me with Bosnich playing.

Incidentally, Kalac has now signed for Roda SC in Holland after failing to get a work permit to play in England. It's much easier to get a work permit in other European countries and there's even talk of changing the system in England. I don't think that would make too much difference because you're only allowed to play three non-EU players anyway. It would just mean they could bring in younger players and the smaller clubs would be able to get in foreigners who aren't internationals. There's loads of good players out there who aren't internationals.

My old club Kaiserslautern has secured the Bundesliga title in Germany. They were only promoted last summer after getting relegated two years ago when I was there.

It's quite an achievement to win the league when you've just come up but I do think that the standard of the German league has dropped. I thought Dortmund were lucky to do so well in the Champions League last season and the other German sides like Bayern Munich, Stuttgart and Schalke 04 have been very inconsistent. Some of the big sides like Moenchengladbach and Cologne have really struggled and look like they could go down.

Kaiserslautern are a side without any stars, they are just a tight, hard-working team. They've only bought about three or four players since I was there. The trainer is the same guy who was there when I left the club - Otto Rehaggel. I don't really rate him because he only buys players who are finished products. Apparently they've signed Uwe Rosler from Manchester City for next season and that's a typical example. He never buys any young players or brings anyone through. Coaching in that situation isn't that difficult.

When I first signed for Kaiserslautern, I was delighted to go there. The previous year they had finished fourth in the league and were in the UEFA Cup. I was told I would be second 'keeper at the club and I trained well. The trainer at the time, Friedel Rausch, and everyone else were raving about me but come the first game I was in the grandstand not on the bench. The 37-year-old Gerrhard Ehrman who was supposed to be goalkeeping coach and third choice was there instead of me.

Eventually he got injured and I was on the bench. Come Christmas we were really struggling and the club was in turmoil. The trainer was under pressure and the first choice 'keeper Andreas Reinke had played 25 games and been very average in all of them. Rausch decided to drop him and put me in. It was a difficult situation to go in to because we desperately needed to win. The first time I played we got a good 1-1 away draw and I played well. I played four games in a row. In the fourth I let in one goal that was my fault in a 3-0 defeat and I never played again.

I was dropped back down to the bench. The trainer told me not to worry about it and that I would get another chance. In Germany, there is a mid-season break after Christmas so I went away for three weeks skiing and so on. When I came back, from day one, Rausch absolutely annihilated me in front of everyone else in training. He verbally abused me all the time. As a young lad, I just couldn't understand it and it was really hard to take.

Fortunately, Rausch was sacked. He went on to Austria and recently took over at Borussia Moenchengladbach who have tailed off second or third last in the league. The new trainer, Eckard Krautzun, was brought in and he seemed to be keen on me. Ehrman got injured and I was on the bench again. We got through to the cup final and a few weeks before, people started saying to me to watch out because a couple of weeks before, Ehrman would make a remarkable recovery, speak to the trainer, sit on the bench and I would be in the stands.

Then, just as people had said, Krautzun came up to me and said that he'd decided to pur Ehrman on the bench. He told me that we needed the points and morale boosting and so on. I played really well in training and in the reserves but, come cup final, I wasn't on the bench.

I felt ripped off. All Ehrman was interested in was collecting his 45,000 DM bonus for winning the final. In the end, he was the one with the bigger mouth and went to the trainer all the time complaining. I'm not the type of person to do that and I don't think that's the right way to behave. I'm a great believer that everyone gets what they deserve in the end and I feel I am now. I don't know whether he has but I'm sure he will some day.

Krautzun was sacked during pre-season of the next campaign and Otto Rehaggel took over. Unfortunately, things didn't get any better and I decided to leave the club after he eventually dropped me from the bench. I went away for a week with the national team to Saudi Arabia and when I came back, after missing one game, I was told I was being dropped from number two to number three. When I asked him why, he said it was because he wanted to see if Ehrman was still up to it - he was 37! I told him I didn't understand and walked out.

In Germany, there's a trainer who picks the team and coaches, and a manager who just looks after contracts and signing players the trainer wants. So I went to see the manager, Hans Peter Briegel, and told him I was very unhappy and wanted to leave. He agreed to let me go.

I watched the Sunderland v Ipswich game at home with my neighbour, who's a Manchester City supporter, as well as Paloma. Before the game, I was thinking this was it. I thought Sunderland would do well to get a draw with Ipswich being on such a good run. I was nervous as hell. On the football pitch, I hardly ever get nervous. I get annoyed when we're not doing anything up front but I hated watching this game knowing we needed them to drop points and I could do nothing about it.

Sunderland started quite well and I thought they might run away with it but Ipswich started to turn it round. I knew it wouldn't end 0-0 so, when Ipswich took the lead, I hit the roof. Then they were all over Sunderland and won a penalty. When they missed it, I got a bad feeling but Ipswich got a second soon after and held on. Sunderland still had some excellent chances to get back into the game but couldn't do it.

The result gives us a huge chance with our game against Wolves tomorrow. We need four points from our last two games and it's all in our hands. I can't see us losing tomorrow and, if I'm right, we'll go into the last game knowing a win will take us up.

April 29th

Boro 1 Wolves 1

We started very nervously and the worst possible thing happened when they got an early goal. It came from a weak clearance which fell to Mark Atkins on the edge of the box. He hit the ball but it was going wide until it hit a divot, curled in and went in off the post. Fortunately, we scored soon afterwards when Hamilton turned and volleyed in.

They had a few chances after that but, in the second half, we ran riot and should really have won the game. It's disappointing not to win but I think most of us are quite happy to get the point. We now need to beat Oxford in the last game. It would have been nice to have had that extra bit of assurance that a draw would be good enough but if that happened and you were level with a few minutes to go, the temptation would be to hang on which would make it a very nervy ending. This way we have to go for it. If someone had told us at the start of the season, we had to beat Oxford at home in our last game to get promoted, we would have taken it.

There's speculation that Australia might try to get the World Cup in 2010. I wouldn't be surprised if we did get it. Everybody loves Australia and would be attracted by the chance to go there.

The facilities would be there with the 2000 Olympics being held in Sydney. With the cricket grounds as well, we would have enough good stadiums around the country. We have a lot of major events and championships in Australia with the golf, tennis, swimming, rugby and cricket. The Olympics is the biggest event in the world so, if we can host that, we could definitely hold the World Cup.

The only question is whether the football authorities could cope with it. As I've said before, they're a Mickey Mouse organisation but there's no reason why they couldn't bring in people who've organised successful tournaments in the past.

Nigel Pearson has announced his retirement from playing. I knew a few months ago that he would pack it in but he never directly told the players. It was just assumed that he would stop playing at the end of the season.

He was going to retire last season but the club talked him into carrying on for another year. You can see why the club wanted to keep him but I thought he would have stopped because his knees are in a bad state. I would hate to see his physical condition in 10 or 20 years time. I told him a couple of weeks ago that, if I was him, I would have given up a few years ago. At the end of the day, your physical health is the most important thing. Nigel and Curtis Fleming have the worst shaped knees in the world.

He wants to go out on a high and if we win promotion against Oxford he will do that. The crowd love him here and, since I've been here, I've seen that, had he been injury-free, he could have gone on to play at a much higher level. He's as good as anyone in the country, even with his bad knees. If he could have steered clear of injuries, I have no doubt he would have played for England.

May 3rd

Boro 4 Oxford United 1

We've done it! For the whole season, we have been fighting to get back into the Premier League and now we have achieved our ambition. It's the best feeling I've ever had in my career.

I moved to Middlesbrough to be in the Premier League. It's the only place to be and, on a personal basis, I want to play there, prove myself and be one of the best 'keepers in the country. Hopefully, that will also help me get back into the national team.

We started the game nervously again and passes weren't finding their targets. It was one of our worst first half performance in months. It was a build-up of tension and going in at 0-0, there were plenty of nerves. In the dressing room at half-time we heard that Sunderland were leading 2-0 and we knew we had to win.

I couldn't believe Alun Armstrong was even playing. We thought he was out for the season with a back injury and didn't know any different until an hour before the game. It worried me that he was in the side for such an important game. He's due to have an operation on his back next week and he didn't look right. He was very cautious and wasn't running right. I wouldn't have played him but you can't argue with the decision because it paid off.

Alun is nothing flash but he is a very accurate finisher. He doesn't get a lot of chances like some other strikers but he puts them away virtually every time. When he scored the first goal I couldn't believe it. It was a great finish and you could sense the relief of everyone on the pitch and in the crowd. Then, a couple of minutes later, Higgy played the ball to Merse and he crossed for Alun to score again. You could sense the pressure lifting off our shoulders. We were 2-0 up, Alun had scored both and I thought - well, that's my judgement out of the window!

Higgy had a good game and scored the third and fourth. After the third, I finally thought "this is it". I could start to enjoy it. I was a bit annoyed to let a goal in near the end but in the last game of the season with four goals up and promotion won, I couldn't get too upset.

After the game, it was a wonderful feeling. It's the longest season I've had, with 45 games including the cup matches, and it has been tremendous. At the start, we had our goal, we needed to get promotion and we've done it.

For me, having experienced two relegations in Germany and coming in for the end of one last season, it's a fantastic feeling to go the other way. No-one can joke about me being an unlucky jinx now. I never saw it that way because I was never really part of the teams that went down but no-one wants to keep suffering that fate.

We only lost nine games all season. I still think we shouldn't have lost that many but we finished with 91 points which is a fantastic total. Four teams were separated by just a few points and all had massive totals compared to previous seasons.

It's unbelievable that Sunderland have finished on 90 points and haven't been promoted. Had we not been automatically promoted, everyone would have been devastated and I don't think we would have won the play-offs. We are all shattered and it would have been very hard to raise ourselves for the games. We have been on good form but so have all the other three sides and I have my doubts.

Looking back now, relegation set us back a year but the club was never in turmoil. I've been at clubs in Germany which have been in turmoil and Middlesbrough was tame by comparison. I'm just glad I didn't join either Manchester City or Everton when I had the chance.

We are a better team now, with players like Merse and Andy Townsend, and with a few quality additions in the summer we can do well in the Premier League. We need to have a good season, not just survive. Clubs like Leicester and Derby have done it and there's no reason why we can't do at least as well as them. We've had two unbelievable seasons and it's all set for another incredible year. Premiership, here we come!